The Great Little Steam Railways of Wales

The Great Little
STEAM RAILWAYS
of Wales

John R. Jones

Commentary by
Anthony Pritchard

Aston Publications Limited

Published in 1991 by Aston Publications Limited
Bourne End House, Harvest Hill,
Bourne End, Bucks SL8 5JJ

First published in 1991.

British Library Cataloguing in Publication Data
Jones, John R.
The great little steam railways of Wales.
1. Wales. Railways
I. Title II. Pritchard, Anthony
385.09429

ISBN 0-946627-64-9

Designed by Chris Hand

Sole distributors to the UK book trade
Springfield Books Limited
Norman Road
Denby Dale
Huddersfield
West Yorkshire
HD8 8TH

Printed in Hong Kong

Contents

Introduction

The narrow-gauge railways of Wales were in the main built for sound commercial reasons in the 19th century, and while the industries that supported them flourished, so did they. When the industries died, so did they, despite attempts to attract tourist traffic in the inter-war years. The death of the slate industry caused the almost casual abandonment of the Ffestiniog and the almost total dereliction of the Talyllyn. Preservation groups fought to save them, their re-birth and revitalization were boosted by the growth of tourism in mid and North Wales and they are now an integral and vigorous component of the Welsh Tourist industry.

Exceptions there are of course and, for example, the Fairbourne became a miniature railway in 1916 and has remained so ever since; the Snowdon Mountain Railway has operated continuously since 1897; the Gwili is a standard-gauge railway over part of the former Great Western route from Carmarthen to Aberystwyth; and the Bala Lake and Llanberis Lake are narrow-gauge lines laid on the track-beds of former wider-gauge systems. Although each railway has its own individual history and character, each is linked by the common thread of industry or tourism.

Although there is a brief history of every railway and every locomotive – this is not a book of history. The aim of John R. Jones – and myself – has been to portray the vibrancy and vitality of Welsh railways today – to capture the locomotives and stock and the operations, scenery and, above all, atmosphere of each of these fiercely independent railway systems.

The writer of the commentary feels able to say, with a minimum of prejudice, that John Jones's photographs are superb and the amount of effort that he put into obtaining unusual and difficult photographs was both immense and planned with detail and precision. Accompanied by his two dogs and, sometimes, stepladder over his shoulder, John has strode for miles over the Welsh countryside to ensure that he was in the right position at the right time for the photograph that he had so patiently planned. Most of the photographs in this book were taken with Leica R5 cameras using Angenieux Zoom lenses of 35 to 70mm and 80 to 210mm. A few photographs were taken with a Rollei 6006 (using Carl Zeiss 55, 80 or 150mm lenses) or with a Fujica 6x7. Where a larger-format camera was used, this is usually indicated in the caption.

We hope that this book will appeal to enthusiasts, modellers and tourists alike.

John R. Jones
Llanidloes

Anthony Pritchard
Ruislip

January 1991

The line closely follows the lakeside with a panorama of views of lake and hillside.

Bala Lake Railway

Until Beeching's axe fell in 1965, one of the most picturesque standard-gauge railway lines in Wales ran from Barmouth Junction (Morfa Mawddach) to Ruabon. There were a number of proposals for preservation of parts of the line, but obviously the section running along the shore of Bala Lake (Llyn Tegid), the largest natural lake in Wales, between Bala and Llanuwchllyn, had the most potential, especially as far as tourist traffic was concerned. The concept was that of local engineer George Barnes and it was supported by the late Tom Jones, Chairman of Merioneth County Council's Finance Committee. In 1971 Rheilffordd Llyn Tegid Cyf (Bala Lake Railway Limited) became the first limited company to be incorporated entirely in the Welsh language. Two years later Cymdeithas Rheilffordd Llyn Tegid (Bala Lake Railway Society) was formed and the railway relies on the Society's volunteers for the operation of the line.

It had been decided to adopt a 1ft 11½in-gauge line, which was laid on the track-bed of the old route. By August 1972 the first 1¼ miles from Llanuwchllyn to Pentrepiod had been opened and month later another three quarters of a mile to Llangower was added. By the start of the 1975 season the line had reached Pant-yr-hen-felin (3 miles), and the remainder of the present section to Bala was opened in 1976. A passing loop at Llangower was opened in 1979 to permit two-train operation during peak periods, the elegant Victorian station at Llanuwchllyn was extended in 1979–80, new locomotive and carriage sheds were erected, the workshop was extended and the station yard was converted into a large car park. There are halts on the line at Pentrepiod Crossing and Flag Station (as it was known by the GWR, but known by British Railways as Glanllyn Halt). The main intermediate station is Llangower, a good point at which to break the journey for a walk. After Bryn Hynod Halt, the line crosses a stream, is carried on a stone embankment through Pant-yr-hen-felin (the site of the 1975 temporary terminus), through a shallow rock cutting lined with heather, perhaps the most beautiful section of this short line, through woods and a cutting and on to the shore of the lake once more before the run to Bala Station. This station, built on the site of the original – opened in 1868 and closed in 1886 – incorporates part of a GWR halt built in 1923 and the waiting shelter from the GWR halt at Llangower. There are plans to build a 4-mile extension to a new terminus much closer to the town centre of Bala.

When the railway first opened, it relied on a small four wheeled diesel-locomotive, the B-B diesel *Meirionnydd*, purpose-built for the line, which joined the Bala Lake in 1973. Regular steam appeared on the line in 1975 with the first of several 0-4-0 saddle-tank locomotives, *Maid Marian*. All have proved very satisfactory and two are in regular service. There are ten passenger coaches, six closed and four open-sided, all purpose-built for the line between 1972 and 1982 and with doors on one side only, because all the platforms are on the lake side of the line. Coaches and stations were painted in a new green and cream livery in 1986.

The ex-Dinorwic Quarry saddletank *Holy War* at Bala Lake Station.

The delightful lake setting, the superb turnout of the little saddle-tank locomotives and the friendly relaxed atmosphere make this one of the most attractive of the Welsh narrow-gauge railways.

Photography: There is plenty of scope for photography, for the line hugs the road alongside the southern shore of the lake for much of its distance. Photographers in the yard at Llanuwchllyn are welcome (provided that they keep off the tracks) and accompanied visits to the sheds are encouraged on request to a Company official or Society member. Several level crossings along the line make good photographic points, as does the brick and iron footbridge at Bala Station.

Other Attractions: The collection of Llanuwchllyn Railway Museum Association is kept in the yard at Llanuwchllyn. It is intended to form the basis of a museum devoted to industrial narrow-gauge railways, and some diesel locomotives and Welsh slate quarry wagons are on display. Llanuwychllyn signal box is open to visitors, with regular demonstrations of signalling equipment and explanations of how the railway is run. Bala Lake makes an excellent centre for visiting Welsh railways.

Holy War **at Llangower, the main intermediate station on the railway.**

Maid Marian takes on water.

Maid Marian shortly before departure from Llanuwchllyn.

Services: Trains run daily from April to September, except on Fridays between certain dates in April, May, June and September. All trains finish their day at Llanuwchllyn, so it is not possible to make a return trip with the last train from Bala. A return trip takes 1 hour. Trains stop to set down by request to the guard at Pentrepiod, Glanllyn and Bryn Hynod halts and to pick up by signalling to the driver. For further information telephone 06784-666 or write to the General Manager, Llanuwchllyn Station, Bala, Gwynedd, LL23 7DD.

The Bala Lake Society is keen to welcome new members interested in supporting the railway. Members receive privilege travel facilities and a quarterly magazine. For details ask at the railway, or contact the Membership Secretary, Mr. P. Briddon, 140 Earl Marshal Road, Sheffield, S4 8LB.

Locomotives

No. 3 Holy War   0-4-0 saddle tank

Built in 1902 by the Hunslet Engine Co. of Leeds, Works No. 779 for shunting in the Dinorwic slate quarry at Llanberis. Taken out of service in 1967, by when it was the last steam locomotive to work in a Welsh slate quarry, and moved to Quainton Road, Aylesbury, for preservation. Purchased by the Rev. Alan Cliff in 1975 and entered service on the Bala Lake in 1979. Bought by Bala Lake Railway Limited in 1989.

No. 5 Maid Marian   0-4-0 saddle tank

Built in 1903 by Hunslet, Works No. 822, for shunting at Dinorwic. Rebuilt on the frame of *Alice*, No. 492 withdrawn in 1964, and bought in 1966 for preservation by the Maid Marian Locomotive Fund. Worked at Bressingham Gardens in Norfolk until 1971, then ran on the Llanberis Lake Railway and joined the Bala Lake in 1975.

No. 11 Meirionnydd   B-B diesel hydrostatic

Purpose-built by Severn Lamb of Stratford upon Avon for the Bala Lake in 1973. Leyland engine. Works regular maintenance trains and occasional special passenger services.

No. 12 Chilmark   Diesel-mechanical

Ruston-Hornsby 40hp built for the Air Ministry in 1940 and used for shunting ammunition at RAF Chilmark in Wiltshire. Acquired in 1976, rebuilt and used on maintenance trains and for shunting.

Through a wooded area about ½ mile from the terminus at Pant. The photograph was taken late in May.

GRAF SCHWERIN-LÖWITZ

Brecon Mountain Railway

The line from Brecon to Newport, originally operated by the Brecon & Merthyr Tydfil Junction Railway, was one of the most scenic in Britain and for much of its length ran within the Brecon Beacons National Park, with superb mountainside views. It encompassed continuous gradients of 1 in 37 for seven miles to Torpantau Tunnel – at 1313ft above sea level the highest tunnel in Great Britain – and then descended over three miles at 1 in 47 to Pontsticill Junction. These splendours did not, however, ensure economic salvation and in 1964 the line was closed by British Railways.

After the track had been lifted, the land was sold off and much of it reverted to sheep grazing. Plans were formulated in 1972 to reopen part of the line as a narrow-gauge tourist railway. In all, 5.5 miles of

Graf Schwerin–Löwitz **heads a Christmas Special, 1989, on the Brecon Mountain Railway.**

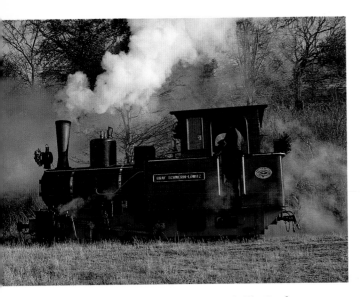

After taking on coal at Pontsticill, *Graf Schwerin–Löwitz* is about to take a Christmas Special back to Pant in 1989.

This photograph was taken further along the line and shows the magnificent views of the Brecon Beacons National Park from the line.

track-bed was acquired from the various owners, but a deviation had to be incorporated because of the impossibility of purchasing one stretch of the original line. The Brecon Beacons National Park Authority supported the new railway and planning permission was granted with the condition that all journeys started outside the park, so that road vehicles can be kept out of the Park.

In June 1980 the first two miles of the 2ft-gauge railway from Pant to Pontsticill were opened after extensive works, which included a new track alignment from Pant Station, the replacement of three bridges which had been removed on closure of the line by British Railways and piping a culvert. At Pant a superb three-storey terminus building incorporating booking office, restaurant, offices and workshops with platform was completed, while at Pontsticill there is a small stone-faced workshop. There are plans to extend the railway along the 2.5-mile-long Taf Fechan Reservoir up to and through Torpantau Tunnel.

The Brecon Mountain Railway has an excellent stud of locomotives, but most of the workload is carried by *Graf Schwerin-Löwitz*, an 0-6-2 tank locomotive. In addition there is a diesel for emergency cover. The carriages on the line, built in the Pant workshops,are based on the frames and bogies of South African Railways freight wagons, each seat 39 or 40 and feature end balconies and observation windows.

Photography: In the National Park there are no photographic problems, and the Pant Terminus is also excellent for photography.

Other Attractions: That the railway is centred on the Brecon Beacons National Park is of course the main attraction.

Services: Commence Sundays only at the beginning of April, run daily over the Easter period and daily from early May through the summer months. Trains do not run on Mondays for much of September and there is a Sunday only service for much of October. For further information telephone 0685-4854 or write to the General Manager, Brecon Mountain Railway, Pant Station, Merthyr Tydfil, Mid Glamorgan, CF48 2UP.

Locomotives

Graf Schwerin-Löwitz   0-6-2 WTT

Built in 1908 by Arn Jung, Jungenthal, Germany, works number 1261, and worked on the 118-mile Mecklenburg–Pommersche Schmalspurbahn. Rebuilt and entered service on the Brecon Mountain Railway in 1981. It is operational in 1991.

4-6-2

Built in 1930 by Baldwin Locomotive Works, Philadelphia, works number 61269, for the Eastern Province Cement Company, Port Elizabeth, South Africa, for operation on their 12-mile New Brighton to Chelsea line. Currently undergoing rebuild.

0-4-0 VBT

Built in 1905 by Mr. Redstone, foreman fitter at the Penmaenmawr Quarry in North Wales, for the son of the owner for use on a garden railway at Plas Mawr, Penmaenmawr. It is 2ft-gauge model of a 3ft-gauge De Winton.

0-4-0 WT

Built in 1936 by Orenstein & Koppel, Berlin, works number 12722, and operated at a stone quarry near Hamburg. Acquired by the Brecon Mountain Railway in 1971.

Pendyffryn   0-4-0 VBT

Built in 1884 by De Winton, Caernarfon, and operated at the Pen-yr-Orsedd Quarry in the Nantlle Valley near Caernarfon.

Sybil   0-4-0 ST

Built in 1903 by Hunslet Engine Co., Leeds, works number 827, for the Pen-yr-Orsedd Slate Quarry Co. Ltd. of Nantlle, near Caernarfon. Operated until the mid-1950s, sold as scrap in 1963, acquired by the Brecon Mountain Railway and rebuilt.

No. 77   2-6-2 + 2-6-2

Built in 1928 by Hanomag, Hannover, works number 10629, the most powerful steam locomotive built for the 2ft-gauge and capable of hauling 600 tons on the level. Initially worked on the Avontuur Railway between Port Elizabeth and Avontuur (177 miles), later worked on the Escourt to Weenan railway in Natal and finally on the Mid-Illovo Railway also in Natal until it closed in 1985. The locomotive was purchased by the Brecon Mountain Railway in 1986.

Now withdrawn from service, *Russell* **on the loop at Penrhyn Point at the Gala Weekend in 1990.**

Fairbourne & Barmouth Steam Railway

For most of its history, this line has been known simply as the Fairbourne Railway. It opened in 1890 as a two-mile 2ft-gauge horse-drawn tramway running from the village of Fairbourne to Penryhn Point, where it linked, and still does, with the ferry to Barmouth. It was originally a horse-drawn tramway, built to carry building materials used in the construction of the village of Fairbourne as a seaside resort. It soon came to be used for carrying passengers and, still horse-drawn, formed a link between Fairbourne Station on the Cambrian Railway, Fairbourne beach and the ferry to Barmouth.

In 1916 the tramway was acquired by Narrow Gauge Railways Limited, a company associated with the Bassett-Lowke Group, the famous model company. Narrow Gauge Railways Limited had been formed in 1911 to take over miniature railways and then develop them on a commercial basis. Under its new ownership the Fairbourne became a miniature railway, so in that respect it was and has remained markedly different from other narrow-gauge railways in Wales, and the track was re-laid to 15in gauge. Initially a Bassett-Lowke miniature 4-4-2 locomotive with open four-wheeled coaches was provided, but in 1925 the line was joined by the famous locomotive *Count Louis*, with the same wheel arrangement and completed in 1923 from parts made in 1914 for racing driver Count Zborowski at his famous country house, Highams, near Canterbury. That same year the railway was sold to Sir Aubrey Brocklebank.

The ownership of the railway changed several times before the Second World War; during the war the railway was closed and it was badly damaged through neglect, the weather and by military operations. New owners acquired the railway in 1946, the track was relaid, the coaches were completely overhauled and the line re-opened the following year with *Count Louis* and a petrol locomotive as motive power units.

Fairbourne–built *No. 24* during early steaming in the summer of 1990 before final painting. This is based on the original *No. 24*, built by the Baldwin company for the former 2ft-gauge Sandy River and Rangeley Lakes Railway in Maine, United States.

Under new ownership *Count Louis* was joined by three new steam locomotives, *Katie* (2-4-2, built by the Guest Engineering and Maintenance Company Limited of Stourbridge in 1954), *Ernest W. Twining* (named after the designer of all three post-war locomotives and acquired in 1961 from Dudley Zoo Railway), and *Siân* (built by the Guest Engineering and Maintenance Company Limited in 1963). The line also had two diesel locomotives, *Rachel* and *Sylvia*.

The line continued to operate successfully from Fairbourne, with halts by request at Bathing Beach Halt and Golf Club Halt (there was a golf club before the war, but it was abandoned because of the encroachment of the sea), to Barmouth Ferry Station, still linking with the ferry to Barmouth and with an extension opened at Penrhyn Point, to bring the line closer to the ferry landing. The operating company became known simply as the Fairbourne Railway Limited in 1958.

In early 1984 the railway was acquired by rock-band leader John Ellerton, who changed the name to the Fairbourne & Barmouth Steam Railway and has operated it through his company, North Wales Narrow Gauge Railways Limited. John Ellerton's ambitions went much further than simply operating railway, and steam locomotive construction was undertaken in the works at Fairbourne. To exploit the potential of locomotive construction, John Ellerton decided to re-lay the track to 12¼in gauge, as this presented far greater commercial prospects for the sale of locomotives. The existing stud of locomotives, together with rolling stock, were disposed of. The venerable *Count Louis* was sold to Tyseley in 1986, *Ernest W. Twining* was sold in Japan, *Siân* was re-built, renamed *Sydney* and sold to Peter de Savary for his railway at Hungerford and *Katie* went to Heyhoe. One of the diesel locomotives was retained and rebuilt to the new gauge.

These have been replaced by a superb new stud of locomotives, *Russell* (modelled on the famous Welsh Highland locomotive), *Beddgelert*, *Sherpa*, *Yeo* (bearing the title *Southern*) and the as yet unnamed S.R.&R.L. No. 24, which was completed for the 1990 season. (The initials stand for Sandy River & Rangeley Lakes Railway.) Sadly *Russell* was badly damaged in a collision with a car in 1989 and this accident distorted the main frame. Although *Russell* steamed at the Gala Weekend in 1990, it has been withdrawn from service for a rebuild and is now not likely to appear again until 1992. The rolling stock is mainly from the Réseau Guerledan Railway, which the Ellertons had operated in Brittany for two years.

John Ellerton is a great publicist and it is now likely that the Fairbourne & Barmouth Railway attracts more publicity than all the other Welsh narrow-gauge railways put together. Bathing Beach Halt was closed. Golf Club Halt was renamed Gorsafawddacha'idraigodanheddogleddollonpenrhynareudraeth-ceredigion (perhaps calculated to gain a place in the *Guinness Book of Records*), Barmouth ferry was renamed Pont Penrhyn and the original Penrhyn Point has been closed. A new loop was completed at Pont Penrhyn in 1990 (where there is an excellent buffet in the Pavilion) to permit through running of trains and a new and very advanced computerized signalling system was introduced. To celebrate the 100th anniversary of the railway in 1990 a horse-drawn tram was reintroduced and, to coincide with this, Bathing Beach Halt was reopened.

Opposite: No. 24 **steaming through Gorsafawddacha'idraigodanheddogleddollonpenrhynareudraeth-ceredigion at the Gala Weekend on the Fairbourne in July 1990.**

Two views of *Sherpa*, modelled on 'the Toy Train' on the Darjeeling railway Northern India. *Sherpa* is at Penrhyn Point.

Sherpa, double-heading with *Southern*, steaming round the loop at Penrhyn Point.

Photography: Because the line is unfenced, photography is easy, and the level crossing at Bathing Beach Halt, the tunnel near Pont Penrhyn and the loop all provide excellent photographic points.

Other Attractions: The railway is set in one of the most attractive Welsh coastal areas and, provided that the weather is not too rough, the crossing to Barmouth on the ferry is highly recommended.

Services: The line operates between early April and late September. Tickets may be bought at Fairbourne and Pont Penrhyn, but there is car parking at Fairbourne only (apart from beach parking). A variety of tickets is available, 1st (dogs banned) and 2nd class, inclusive of the Ferry if wished and to include lunch in the Pavilion on Sundays during May, June and September. For further information telephone 0341-250362 or write to Fairbourne & Barmouth Steam Railway, Beach Road, Fairbourne, Gwynedd, LL38 2PZ.

Locomotives

Name	Wheel Arrangement	Date of Construction	Name of Constructor
Russell	2-6-4T	1979	Milner Engineering, Rebuilt 1986
Beddgelert	0-6-4T	1979	David Curwen, Rebuilt 1987
Sherpa	0-4-0	1978	Milner Engineering, Rebuilt 1988
Yeo	2-6-2T	1978	David Curwen, Rebuilt 1989
No. 24	2-6-2	1990	Fairbourne Locomotive Works
Lilian Walter (diesel)	A1-1A	1985	Fairbourne Locomotive Works

Opposite above: Southern (also known as *Yeo*) was another locomotive built in the small workshops at Fairbourne. It is also seen on the loop at Penrhyn Point at the Gala Weekend. Barmouth Harbour is in the background.

Opposite below: With a goods train specially constructed for the 1990 Gala Weekend, *Beddgelert* steams away at the Gala Weekend. Barmouth Railway bridge is in the background. The structure to the right is a water tower.

On the Cei Mawr. *Moultaineer* on the 62ft-high dry-stone embankment. At the end of the 1990 season the trees were extensively thinned to permit photographs from an angle not possible for many years. Compare this photograph with the photograph of *Linda* on the Cei Mawr on the front cover.

Ffestiniog Railway

Longest of the surviving narrow-gauge railways in Wales, the Ffestiniog has enjoyed a significant but chequered history, closely linked with and dependent on the development of what was a remote mountain area. William Alexander Madocks, the MP for Boston in Lincolnshire, had acquired land on the shores of Traeth Mawr, a tidal estuary into which the River Glaslyn flowed. Madocks loved the wildness of North Wales, but was determined to tame it by far-sighted and ambitious plans for land reclamation. These led to the construction of the Cob, completed in 1811, a vast embankment that sealed the mouth of the estuary and diverted the Glaslyn, which began to scour an ever-deepening channel. Madocks determined to exploit what nature was already doing and work was put in hand to build Port Madoc (named after Madocks and not Prince Madoc and now known as Porthmadog), which was completed in 1824.

Throughout the 19th century the Welsh slate industry grew and developed until it played a major role in the Principality's employment and economy. Slate deposits in the mountains around Blaenau Ffestiniog, about 13 miles to the north-east of Port Madoc, were mined in small quantities, transported by pack animals and farm carts to the River Dwyryd, by shallow-draught river boats to Traeth Bach and then transferred to sea-going sailing ships. It was only too obvious that transportation difficulties limited production. Rival plans were promoted for a rail connection to the sea and the successful proposal, the Festiniog Railway (note, legally, not Ffestiniog, although the latter spelling is now always used), was incorporated by Act of Parliament on 23 May, 1832.

A gauge of 1ft 11½in was chosen, the same as in the slate quarries, wide enough for horses to work without difficulty and narrow enough for the line to negotiate the sharp curves made unavoidable by the mountainous route. James Spooner was contracted to survey the line and be responsible for the construction of the railway. The line was opened in 1836, descending some 700ft from Blaenau Ffestiniog, then still a village, to the Cob, with an almost level crossing of the Cob to Porthmadog Station. For many years the slate trains descended the line by gravity (with the horses that originally pulled the empty trains up the line riding and feeding in 'dandy' cars). Initially business was poor, only one slate mine committed itself to use the line, but its value gradually became apparent and eventually 10 slate mines used the line.

With a journey time of two hours down to Porthmadog, eight hours up empty, trains of over 300 yards long (100-plus wagons) and a schedule of six or seven trains a day, the operation of the line was coming under increasing pressure. In addition there was demand for a passenger service. After control of the line had been acquired by Charles Easton Spooner (James Spooner's son) in 1856, plans were put in hand for steam operation and a passenger service. In October 1863 *The Princess* and *Mountaineer* entered service and they were joined by *The Prince* and *Palmerston* in 1864, when the Railway received permission from the Board of Trade to operate passenger trains.

**Carriage-building at Boston Lodge.
The carriage is being panelled with
aluminium cladding.**

Linda **in the works at Boston Lodge.**

Although an Act of Parliament authorizing the doubling of the line and other changes was passed in 1869, the cost was prohibitive. The combined problems of improving capacity on the line by using longer and heavier trains that required greater motive power and using more powerful locomotives that could negotiate the line's sharp curves and climb the steep ascents was solved in 1870. The Ffestiniog took delivery of *Little Wonder*, the first of Robert Fairlie's narrow-gauge patent 'double-engines', looking like two engines back-to-back, but in fact with a single long boiler, central fireboxes and driving position, coal and water stored adjacent and the whole mounted on twin powered bogies. Improved versions followed, *James Spooner* (1872), *Taliesin* (a single powered bogie version in 1876); *Merddin Emrys* (1879) and *Livingston Thompson* (1886) followed and both were built by the Company in its works at Boston Lodge. Bogie passenger coaches and goods wagons were adopted from 1872 onwards. By the late 1870s the Ffestiniog's slate business was threatened by the London & North Western Railway and the Great Western, which extended lines to gain access to the exchange quarries of the slate mines. For many years the loss of slate traffic was compensated for by the growth in tourism. After the First World War the slate Industry declined rapidly, the result of the gain in popularity of other roofing materials, accelerated by major strikes within the industry. The Railway became increasingly dependent on tourism throughout the 1920s and 1930s.

Merddin Emrys **at Porthmadog Station. An original Fairlie locomotive, built in 1879, it is painted in 1880s livery.**

Merddin Emrys and *Mountaineer* at Porthmadog Station during the 1990 Gala Weekend.

Mountaineer, brought back from France and acquired by the Ffestiniog Railway in 1967, leaves Porthmadog with a train for Blaenau Ffestiniog.

With Porthmadog harbour in the background, *Linda* and *Mountaineer* double-headed across the Cob with a train for Blaenau Ffestiniog during the 1990 Gala Weekend.

On the Cob just before the Toll House, *Linda* approaches Boston Lodge works.

No. 2, *Prince*, built in 1863/4 for the Ffestiniog, and the oldest narrow-gauge railway locomotive in Wales still in steam, is seen at Minffordd Crossing.

Linda, an ex-Penrhyn Quarry locomotive, first loaned to the Ffestiniog in 1962 and bought in 1963, at Minffordd Station.

Passenger services ceased on 15 September, 1939, following the declaration of war on Germany. Throughout the war years the Railway continued to operate slate traffic on a modest scale, but the quarries came to rely increasingly on road transport and there was no money for repair and renovation of the track and rolling stock. By 1945 the Ffestiniog had sold all the land that it could in Porthmadog to raise cash, the service was down to three days a week and only about 50 tons of slate a week was being carried. Appeals for financial assistance from the mines went unheeded (they were almost totally using the roads and the main railway line by this time) and on 1 August, 1946, services ceased, and the line, buildings and rolling stock were abandoned (but not legally, as that would have required an Act of Parliament).

It was not until 1951 that serious steps were taken to see whether the Railway could be restored. In 1954, Alan Pegler acquired a controlling interest in the Ffestiniog (later his shares were transferred to the Ffestiniog Railway Trust). The volunteer directors and enthusiasts, together with a small number of paid employees, started on reconstruction. Using the Railway's Simplex tractor, a passenger service from Porthmadog to Boston Lodge started on 23 July, 1955, the restored *Prince* soon took over the duties and the service was gradually extended. By May 1956 trains ran as far as Minffordd; they reached Penrhyn by April 1957 and Tan-y-Bwlch in April 1958.

Earl of Merioneth on the Cutting Naddu. This Fairlie locomotive, built at Boston Lodge Works in 1979, was the first Fairlie to be built since 1911.

The Cutting Naddu is a shelf hewn on the hillside and is in the Coed Cae Fali wood. This photograph of *Linda* was taken at ground level using a step ladder. This point on the line can be reached by a path through the wood.

Mountaineer near Cutting Budr, with a superb view across the valley to the River Dwyryd. This photograph shows the full autumnal splendour of the Welsh landscape.

Early summer on the Ffestiniog. *Linda* in the woods at Sheepfold Curve. The overhanging trees cause shutter speed problems. The widest possible aperture (in this case with a 50mm F2 Leitz lens) and slow shutter speed (here 1/125 on 200 ASA film) are needed.

Taken from a stone overhang above the line, *Linda* is seen on Tyler's Curve heading back to Porthmadog.

Mountaineer on the embankment above Plas Tan-y-Bwlch, approaching Tyler's Curve.

It was always planned to reopen the line right through to Blaenau Ffestiniog, but these plans had already been thwarted. The North Wales Hydro-Electric Act, 1955, promoted by the then British Electricity Authority, authorized a scheme for upper and lower reservoirs, with a pumping and generating station near Tanygrisiau, and despite the Railway's opposition, this resulted in the compulsory purchase of the line above Moelwyn Tunnel. The railway planned an alternative route to the east of the reservoir linked by a spiral from Dduallt, running over the crest of the dam and rejoining the original line at Tanygrisiau. It was a magnificent, ambitious plan for a railway that had been treated with disdain and abruptly told 'to go and play with your trains' at the Select Committee of the House of Lords in 1955.

Whilst work started on the deviation from the original route over land given to the Railway by the Economic Forestry Group, the line was reopened to Dduallt in 1968. The Dduallt deviation was completed in 1971 and the Moelwyn Tunnel in 1977, and Llyn Ystradau became the temporary terminus of the line. By 1978 trains could run as far as Tanygrisiau and the final mile of the line, reinstated with the co-operation of Gwynedd County Council, who agreed a revised road scheme to permit the building of the line to the centre of Blaenau Ffestiniog, was completed in 1982. The new

Opposite: *Merddin Emrys* on Tyler's Curve, which was named after Henry Tyler, of the Railway Inspectorate. Note the guard-rail on the curve.

joint station of British Rail and the Ffestiniog is on the site of the old Ffestiniog and Great Western Station opened in 1883. With the hard-fought completion of the line, the Ffestiniog became truly the 'Jewel in the Crown' of Welsh narrow-gauge railways. Control of the railway remains with the Ffestiniog Railway Trust. All steam locomotives on the line have been oil-burning since the mid-1970s, using a mixture of waste oil and diesel oil, necessary because of the need to prevent the risk of sparks causing fire in the forests of the Forestry Commission through which so much of the line passes. *Linda* was experimentally converted to 'gas producer' coal burning for a short period.

Although the Railway was built to carry slate from Blaenau Ffestiniog to Porthmadog, and that was its traditional 'direction', most passengers join the train at Porthmadog, and it is now more accurately regarded as running from Porthmadog to Blaenau Ffestiniog.

Linda between the conifers on Whistling Curve. A difficult shot because of the massive shadows thrown by the trees when the sun is out.

This view of *Prince* taking on water at Tan-y-Bwlch shows to good effect the proportions of the Ffestiniog's most historic locomotive.

Above: Merddin Emrys **takes on water at Tan-y-Bwlch. This photograph was taken with flash.**

A Journey

Any passenger with a more than passing interest in the line cannot but buy the Ffestiniog Railway's *Traveller's Guide*, which contains a detailed annotated map that forms a fine history of the railway's fortunes and misfortunes.

Although there is a station car park at Porthmadog, it is overcrowded at peak times, but there is more than adequate municipal parking within a couple of hundred yards. Porthmadog grew rapidly with the railway and the slate industry, died equally swiftly with their downfall and is now once again a pleasant and revitalized seaside town. Porthmadog Harbour Station is in part original, but it has been substantially rebuilt and extended to incorporate first floor offices, 'The Little Wonder' refreshment bar and give access to the Ffestiniog Railway museum which occupies the old goods shed. From the station the line crosses the Cob, with magnificent views across the sandbanks of Traeth Mawr (Great Sand) to Snowdonia and Boston Lodge. Named after Madocks' parliamentary constituency in Lincolnshire, this was the site of a quarry for the stone used in the construction of the Cob. Boston Lodge acted as the office, stables and barracks during construction and subsequently became the site of the Ffestiniog's locomotive works, which can be seen to the right of the track.

The 2-mile mark is reached at Minffordd, a station beside the main A487 road and an interchange with British Rail's Cambrian Coast Line. At Penrhyn, just over three miles, the railway enters the Snowdonia National Park, and now, for most of the way to Dduallt, just under the 10-mile mark, the line runs on the shelf of the hillside, gaining height above the valley, and with spectacular views reaches Rhiw Goch, just over 4 miles. Then on to Plas Halt, through Whistling Curve (where up trains used to whistle to warn of their approach to Tan-Y-Bwlch), across the magnificent cast-iron skew bridge, originally built at Boston Lodge in 1854, to Tan-Y-Bwlch, where all trains stop. A nature trail can be reached from Tan-Y-Bwlch station. Between Tan-Y-Bwlch and Garnedd Tunnel there are superb views of Llyn Mair (Mary's Lake).

Just before Dduallt the line passes under the spiral deviation and as it leaves the station swings east into the spiral that climbs 35ft to allow the line to pass to the west of Ffestiniog power station. The line branches away from the old 1836 route, through the new Moelwyn Tunnel opened in 1977, past the Tanygrisiau Reservoir and the power station. Just before Tanygrisiau there are magnificent falls to the west of the line. Waste slate tips tower above the line as it approaches Blaenau Ffestiniog, where it passes high above the houses on the outskirts of the town, between the backs of the town's houses where sheep roam freely and swings south to run parallel with the British Rail line into the terminus.

On a first journey on the Ffestiniog there is simply too much to absorb and it takes several trips to develop a feel for the line.

Mountaineer exiting from the 60-yard Garnedd Tunnel.

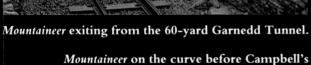

Mountaineer on the curve before Campbell's Platform, a halt by request opened in 1968.

Merddin Emrys as *Mountain Prince* on the embankment after the Garnedd Tunnel.

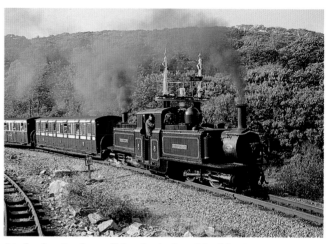

Linda in front of the signalling hut at Dduallt.

At the beginning of the deviation *Merddin Emrys* passes the siding used for diesel works trains.

On the deviation, *Earl of Merioneth* heads the Vintage Special, a train of historic carriages, during the Gala Weekend in 1990.

Rolling Stock

The Ffestiniog Railway has in its rolling stock a vast array of passenger coaches, including some early four-wheelers. Four of these, together with one in the Museum, were built for the Ffestiniog in 1963–4 by Brown Marshall & Co. of Birmingham and are the survivors of the first passenger-carrying vehicles on a narrow-gauge railway, probably in the world and certainly in Great Britain. Only one is in service at the moment, together with a four-wheel quarrymen's carriage built by the Ffestiniog in 1885/6. One is undergoing restoration and with another two restoration is pending. Apart from a number of 19th-century bogie coaches, including the first bogie passenger coaches in regular service in Great Britain, the company has a wide range of coaches built at Boston Lodge Works from 1964 onwards.

At the top of the deviation, *Mountaineer* heads back towards Porthmadog.

Linda and ***Earl of Merioneth*** **double-head a Blaenau Ffestiniog train through a bend in the woods above the deviation. The photograph was taken at the 1990 Gala Weekend.**

Above the deviation *Linda* on the straight approaching the 287-yard Moelwyn Tunnel, opened in June 1977.

A Vintage Special hauled by *Earl of Merioneth* by the side of Tanygrisiau Reservoir. The front endpaper gives a view of *Linda* above the Reservoir.

A train from Blaenau Ffestiniog hauled by *Merddin Emrys* approaches the power station.

Merddin Emrys approaches the falls before Tanygrisiau.

Linda at the falls before Tanygrisiau. Usually the spate of the falls is not so heavy.

Mountaineer and *Linda* at Tanygrisiau Station, double-heading for Porthmadog.

Linda **heading towards Tanygrisiau Station from the Dolrhedyn Bridge with a Porthmadog train.**

Photography: On the Ffestiniog photography falls into three categories, a 'doddle', difficult and dangerous. Nothing can be easier than taking photographs at any of the stations or on the spiral loop, which is ideal. There are, however, a vast number of other points on the line at which photographs can be taken safely. It is a matter of studying the Ordnance Survey sheet and working your way across country through woods and along footpaths that can be legitimately used. Some of the photographs in this book were taken safely from places where most photographers do not even know places exist. The third category is DANGEROUS. NEVER, EVER attempt to use the line to reach a photographic point. At many places on the line the clearance between train and wall is only inches and the trains cannot stop quickly.

Other Attractions: At Porthmadog there is the nascent Welsh Highland Railway, the Porthmadog Maritime Museum, Porthmadog harbour and, nearby, the Italianate village of Portmeirion. The Llechwedd tourist centre, with displays and tours of the old slate workings, and Gloddfa Ganol Slate Mine are easily reached from Blaenau Ffestiniog Station.

Above the roof tops of Blaenau Ffestiniog with the Chapel to the left of *Linda*.

Below: Mountaineer **at the level crossing at Glan-y-Pwll shortly before Blaenau Ffestiniog. As is only too evident from this photograph, this is one of the wettest areas in Wales.**

Services: Trains run Saturdays and Sundays only for much of March and there is then a daily service through to early November. In addition, there are Father Christmas Specials during December, and there is a daily service from Boxing Day to New Year's Day. Depending on the location of winter track repairs a diesel push-pull heated train operates on certain days during November and February. For further information telephone 0766-512340 (Porthmadog) or 0766-831654 (Blaenau Ffestiniog) or write to The Ffestiniog Railway, Porthmadog, Gwynedd, LL49 9NF.

Locomotives

In Service

No. 2 Prince   0-4-0 STT

This was one of the first four locomotives built for the railway by G. England & Co and delivered in 1864. It was originally named *The Prince*. It was the first locomotive in steam when the railway was preserved, and had been assembled with a boiler delivered in 1945. It was rebuilt in 1980 with superheated boiler and oil burning.

No. 10 Merddin Emrys   0-4-4-0 T

Fairlie Patent double-bogie locomotive designed and built at Boston Lodge Works in 1879. Fitted with new superheated boiler from Hunslet Engine Co., Leeds, in 1970, converted to oil burning in 1972 and is now painted in 1880s livery.

Earl of Merioneth/Iarll Merionnydd   0-4-4-0 T

Fairlie Patent double-bogie locomotive designed and built at Boston Lodge Works in 1979 (the first Fairlie built since 1911), using the bogies from *Livingston Thompson* (which was also named *Earl of Merioneth/Iarll Merionnydd* between 1961–71).

Linda   2-4-0 STT

Built for Penrhyn Quarry Railway as 0-4-0ST by the Hunslet Engine Co., works number 590, in 1893. Loaned to the Ffestiniog in 1962, ownership acquired 1963 and rebuilt as 2-4-0STT in 1970.

Blanche   2-4-0 STT

Built for Penrhyn Quarry Railway as 0-4-0 ST by the Hunslet Engine Co., works number 589, in 1893. Acquired 1963, rebuilt as 2-4-0 STT in 1972. Not in service

Mountaineer   2-6-2 T

Built for War Dept Light Railways, France, by American Loco Co., Paterson, New Jersey, works number 57156, in 1917. Used in France from 1935 on the Tramway de Pithiviers à Toury until its closure at the end of 1964. Brought to the UK and donated to the Ffestiniog Railway in 1967. Modified to Ffestiniog loading gauge in 1967, oil burning in 1971, new superheated boiler, etc., in 1982, new cab, etc., in 1983. Carries replicas of the name-plates of the original *Mountaineer* delivered to the Ffestiniog in 1863.

Not in service

No. 1 Princess	**0-4-0 STT**

Built for the Ffestiniog by G. England and delivered in 1863, the first steam locomotive for a public narrow-gauge railway. Operated last train before the closure of the line on 1 August, 1946. Exhibited at Blaenau Ffestiniog 1969–80, took part in the Stockton & Darlington 150th anniversary celebrations in 1975 and after partial restoration in 1981 exhibited in the Ffestiniog Railway Museum.

No. 5 Welsh Pony	**0-4-0 STT**

Fifth locomotive built for the Ffestiniog by G. England and delivered in 1867. Major overhauls in 1891 and 1915. Boiler condemned in 1938. Now owned by the Ffestiniog Railway Trust and displayed outside Porthmadog Harbour Station. A larger and more powerful design than the first four built for the railway.

No. 3 Livingston Thompson	**0-4-4-0 T**

Fairlie Patent double-bogie locomotive designed and built at Boston Lodge Works in 1886. Major overhauls in 1905, 1932 and 1956. Named *Taliesin* 1932–61 and *Earl of Merioneth/Iarll Meirinnydd* 1961–71. Withdrawn in October 1971. Name transferred to the new Fairlie built at Boston Lodge Works in 1979. Restored cosmetically in 1988 to 1910 period and on long-term loan for display in the National Railway Museum, York. Owned by the Ffestiniog Railway Trust.

0-4-0 + 0-4-0-0 T

The first Beyer-Garratt patent articulated locomotive and built by Beyer, Peacock & Co., Manchester, works number 5792, in 1909 for N.E. Dundas Tramway, Tasmania. Line closed in 1929, returned to Beyer, Peacock in 1947 and kept at their works until 1966, when acquired by fund-raising for the Ffestiniog. Stored pending modifications, but on long-term loan for display in the National Railway Museum, York, since 1976. Owned by the Ffestiniog Railway Trust.

Privately owned

Britomart	**0-4-0 ST**

Built by the Hunslet Engine Co., works number 707, in 1899 for the Pen-yr-Orsedd Quarry. After major overhaul in 1966, steamed on the Ffestiniog. Overhauled again in 1982. Coal-fired.

Palmerston	**0-4-0 STT**

Built by G. England & Co. for the Ffestiniog and entered service in 1864. Rebuilt in 1888 as the first England locomotive to have an enclosed cab and an all-over tank in place of the original side tanks. Major overhaul in 1910. From 1923 worked on both the Ffestiniog Railway and the Welsh Highland Railway. Taken out of service in 1940, but used to supply steam to Boston Lodge Works. In 1974 it was sold to the Palmerston Locomotive Group and is undergoing long-term restoration.

On the bend before the road bridge, *Earl of Merioneth* heads into Blaenau Ffestiniog Station

Mountaineer and *Merddin Emrys* at Blaenau Ffestiniog Station.

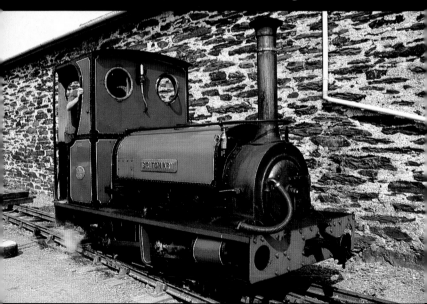

Britomart in steam at the demonstration area at Minfford Crossing.

Diesel Locomotives

Mary Ann	**4-Wheel Diesel Mechanical**

Built by Motor Rail Ltd., Bedford, in 1917 for War Dept Light Railways, France, sold to Kent Construction & Engineering Co., Ashford, and acquired by the Ffestiniog in 1923. It was the first locomotive restored to working order (1954), worked the first passenger train on 23 July, 1955, fitted name plates 1971 and overhauled again in 1973, when the cab was added. Fitted with Gardner 4LK engine in place of the original 40hp Dorman petrol. It bears works plate number 596, but it seems that this was fitted from another Simplex at Ashford in 1923, and it does not really relate to this locomotive.

Moelwyn	**2-4-0 Diesel Mechanical**

Built by Baldwin Loco Works, Philadelphia (or may have been sub-contracted), works number 49604, in 1918 for French Government Artillery Railways. Subsequently acquired by E. W. Farrow & Sons, Spalding, and bought by the Ffestiniog in 1925. Overhauled in 1956 and fitted with Gardner diesel engine (in place of the original 45hp Pittsburgh petrol). Rebuilt as 2-4-0 DM in 1957 and overhauled again in 1966.

Ashover	**4-Wheel Diesel Mechanical**

Built by F. C. Hibberd, Park Royal, works number 3307, in 1948 for the Ashover Light Railway and after passing through several hands was acquired by the Ffestiniog Railway in late 1981. Major overhaul 1987–8. Perkins 48hp engine.

Upnor Castle	**4-Wheel Diesel Mechanical**

Built by F. C. Hibberd, Park Royal, works number 3687, in 1954 for the Chattenden & Upnor Railway, Chatham. This Royal Navy line closed in 1960. In 1962 the locomotive was acquired by the Welshpool & Llanfair Light Railway and became No. 4, *Upnor Castle*. Acquired by the Ffestiniog Railway in 1968. After being cut down and re-gauged from 2ft 6in to 2ft 0in, entered service in August 1968. Re-engined in 1971 and 1980 and now fitted with 180hp Gardner engine.

Conway Castle/Castell Conwy	**4-Wheel Diesel Mechanical**

Built by F. C. Hibberd, Park Royal, works number 3831, in 1958 for the Royal Naval Armaments Depot at Ernesettle, Plymouth. Acquired by the Ffestiniog Railway in May 1981 and regauged from 2ft 6in to 2ft 0in. When overhauled at Boston Lodge in 1985–6 fitted with new superstructure. Gardner 180hp engine.

Moel Hebog   0-4-0 Diesel Mechanical

Built by the Hunslet Co. for the National Coal Board, works number 4113, in 1955 and worked at New Stubbin Colliery, Dewsbury, Yorkshire. Re-gauged to 2ft 0in on transfer to Shaw Colliery, Rawmarsh, Yorks. Acquired by the Ffestiniog Railway in 1969, rebuilt in 1975 when it was fitted with a cab and name plates added. Meadows 70hp engine.

Harlech Castle   0-6-0 Diesel Hydraulic

Built by Baguley-Drewry Ltd., Burton-on-Trent, works number 3736 for Instituto Nacional do Acucar, Mozambique, but not delivered. Used by the Ffestiniog Railway on trial in 1895, returned to the makers in 1986 and acquired in 1988. Caterpillar 140hp engine. Re-entered service with P.W. Dept and named 1990.

Jane (formerly)   4-Wheel Diesel Mechanical

Built by Motor Rail Ltd., Bedford, works number 8565, in 1940 for St. Albans Sand & Gravel Co. Acquired by Colonel Campbell in 1966 and passed to the Ffestiniog Railway in 1971. The name was carried from 1972 to 1976 and it retains the original Dorman 20hp engine. It is out of use.

The Colonel   4-Wheel Diesel Mechanical

Built by Motor Rail Ltd., Bedford, works number 8788, in 1943 for St. Albans Sand & Gravel Co. Acquired by Colonel Campbell in 1943 and by the Ffestiniog Railway in 1982, when it was named in his memory. Dorman 20hp engine.

Diana   4-Wheel Diesel Mechanical

Built by Motor Rail Ltd., Bedford, works number 21579, in 1957 for Minworth Sewage Works, Birmingham, and was delivered to the Ffestiniog Railway at Glan-y-Pwll in August 1974. It was named two months later. The engine is a 20hp Dorman.

Alistair   4-Wheel Diesel Mechanical

Built by Ruston & Hornsby, Lincoln, works number 201970, in 1949 for Bierrum & Partners and given to the railway in 1968. Ruston 13hp engine. Not in use.

Stefcomatic   2-2-0 Diesel Hydraulic

Built as a standard-gauge self-propelled ballast tamping machine by Matisa, Switzerland, works number 48589, in 1956 and delivered to British Railways (Southern Region). Acquired by the Ffestiniog Railway 1968, but did not enter service until 1978, when it had been rebuilt and re-gauged to 2ft 0in.

Ex-Dinorwic Quarry 0-4-0 *Elidir* **at Llanberis Lake Station.**

Llanberis Lake Railway

Although the Llanberis Lake Railway, one of the most scenic railways in Wales, was not opened until 1971, its origins lie, like so many other Welsh railways, in the flourishing slate industry that grew in importance throughout the 19th century. The Dinorwic Quarry Company operated at Llanberis on Elidir Mountain what became the largest slate quarry in the world and at one stage employed 3000 men. From 1843 to 1961 the 4ft-gauge Padarn Railway carried slate from Dinorwic Quarry to a private harbour at Y Felinheli on the Menai Straits between Bangor and Caernarfon known as Port Dinorwic. Another 1ft 10¾in gauge system, mainly operated by Hunslet 0-4-0 saddle-tanks, served the quarry complex. Dinorwic Quarry Company survived until 1969, when it went into liquidation and three steam locomotives from the 1ft 10¾in system, together with some diesels and the rest of the company's assets, were auctioned.

Another view of *Elidir* with a train alongside the lake. The line gives beautiful views of the Snowdonia range of mountains.

Thomas Bach, also known as *Wild Aster*, heading along the lakeside.

Another ex-Dinorwic Quarry locomotive, *Dolbadarn*, hauls a train back to Llanberis Lake Station.

Already the Llanberis Lake Railway Society had been formed and it made a successful bid for the three steam locomotives and one diesel. The land owned by the quarry became a vast natural Country Park and the quarry's extensive Victorian workshops were developed as the National Slate Museum of Wales. The River Authority had acquired much of the track-bed of the 4ft-gauge railway along Padarn Lake, the balance was acquired by Caernarfon County Council and the entire length was leased to Rheilffordd Llyn Padarn Cyf (Padarn Lake Railway Ltd.), together with the locomotive shed. The new company decided to re-lay the track to the more common 1ft 11½in gauge (rather than the quarry's 1ft 10¾in) using some rails from the quarry system and the motive power bought at the auction was suitably modified. A new station was built at Llanberis, blending in with a small complex of craft workshops built nearby and with excellent parking facilities.

The first section of the line from Llanberis to Cei Llydan was scheduled to open on 28 May, 1971, but shortly before the opening ceremony it was discovered that a section of the line had settled under the weight of the locomotive *Dolbadarn*. As a result public passenger services did not start until 19 July, 1971, and in 1972 the line was extended to its present terminus at Penllyn.

All trains start from and terminate at Llanberis station. The line, after leaving the Station, runs between slate tips that form a deep cutting, under a high stone archway built in 1900 and out on to the lakeside with its superb view across the lake to Llanberis village and Snowdon. For the remainder of its 2-mile length the line hugs the lakeside. Cei Llydan Station is the half-way point; the train runs through without stopping on its outbound journey and there is a loop so that trains can pass each other in the station. There follows Volcano Cutting, with rocks formed by solidified lava from an extinct volcano, and the train then passes a substantial slate building on the right-hand side of the line. This is a water pumping plant for the hydro-electric generating station built within Elidir Mountain beneath the Dinorwic Quarry workings – the pumping station draws water from the lake to cool power cables laid underground beside the railway. At Penllyn the locomotive reverses round the loop and takes the train back to Llanberis. On the return trip the train stops at Cei Llydan, an ideal picnic site. The round trip takes 40 minutes.

The railway operates three Hunslet saddle-tanks, all ex-Dinorwic Quarry, together with two Ruston-Hornsby diesels that from time to time haul passengers and a number of diesels used for maintenance of the track and the underground power cables laid alongside the line. There is a total stock of 13 passenger coaches, all built specially for the line, and the majority built in the museum workshop. Five of the coaches are fully enclosed 30-seaters, plus two similar coaches and six 21-seat coaches fully glazed but lacking doors and used in fine weather. All the coaches have entrances on one side only, as all platforms are on the inland side of the line.

Photography: Whilst not a difficult line to photograph, open for most of its length, particularly useful points are the archway at Llanberis and Cei Llydan Station.

Other Attractions: The line is set within the splendour of Snowdonia, close to the Snowdon Mountain Railway and the Llanberis path to the summit of Snowdon. Footpaths are laid out through the oak-clad hillside at Llanberis. The National Slate Museum of Wales is a 'must' to visit.

Services: Trains operate on Mondays to Thursdays from March to October, also on Fridays, Saturdays and Sundays during the busier months. For further information telephone 0286-870549 or write to the Traffic Manager, Padarn Lake Railway Ltd., Gilfachddu, Llanberis, Caernarfon, Gwynedd, LL55 4TY.

Elidir **just before the middle point on the line, Cei Llyden.**

Locomotives

No. 1 Elidir   0-4-0 Saddle Tank

Built in 1889 by the Hunslet Engine Co. of Leeds, Works No. 493, for the Dinorwic Quarry. Originally named *Enid*, renamed *Red Damsel*. Taken out of service for overhaul in 1957, work not completed and acquired dismantled by the Llanberis Lake Railway in 1969. Overhauled, fitted with cab from another locomotive, *Irish Mail*, and entered service in 1971.

No. 2 Wild Aster   0-4-0 Saddle Tank

Built in 1904 by Hunslet, Works No. 849, for the Dinorwic Quarry. Originally No. 7 (no name), but later named *Wild Aster*. Taken out of service in 1961, acquired by the Llanberis Lake Railway in 1969 and entered service in 1988. Currently carries the name *Thomas Bach*.

No. 3 Dolbadarn   0-4-0 Saddle Tank

Built in 1922 by Hunslet, Works No. 1430, for shunting at Port Dinorwic. Originally No. 2 (no name). Transferred to the Dinorwic Quarry in 1936 and named *Dolbadarn* in 1946. Remained in service at the quarry until 1967, acquired by the Llanberis Lake Railway in 1969 and entered service in 1971.

No. 4 Una   0-4-0 Saddle Tank

Also built by Hunslet and of similar design to the above locomotives. Maintained in full working order at the Slate Museum, but operates from time to time on the railway.

No. 8 Twll Coed   Diesel

Ruston-Hornsby 48hp built in 1952 and used for hauling ammunition trains, including the Chattenden & Upnor Railway in Kent operated by the Admiralty and which closed in 1961. Sent for scrap to Wood Pit Colliery, Lancashire, acquired by the Llanberis Lake Railway in 1976 and rebodied.

Snowdon Mountain Railway

In contrast with other Welsh railways, the Snowdon Mountain Railway, Britain's only public rack-and-pinion railway, has enjoyed an uncomplicated, straightforward history – except for its first day of operation. The Snowdon Mountain Tramroad and Hotels Company Limited (now Snowdon Mountain Railway Plc) was incorporated in 1894 to build a railway from Llanberis to the summit of Snowdon. Snowdonia was by this time a major tourist area, Beddgelert was rapidly becoming its focal point and the aim was to put Llanberis back on the map. Work started in December 1894 on the 4¾ mile line, which has a vertical climb of 3150ft. The line is single track with passing places at Hebron, Halfway Station and Clogwyn. Laid to a gauge of 800mm (2ft 7½in), it is fitted throughout with a double-bladed rack to the design patented by the Swiss Engineer Dr. Roman Abt in 1882. The locomotives always run chimney-first up the mountain, pushing the coach in front. The coach is not coupled to the locomotive. Locomotives and coaches have independent automatic brakes.

No. 2, *Enid*, at Llanberis Station, about to position itself behind the carriage. In the mist can be seen the Dinorwic Quarry slate tips.

Enid between Hebron Station and Halfway Station.

The Llanberis shed with locomotives *Ralph* and *Eryri*. All Snowdon locomotives have inclined boilers so that the boilers are more or less level on the ascent and descent.

The construction of the line was a magnificent engineering achievement, accomplished in a remarkably short space of time, with no level sections and a steepest gradient of 1 in 5.5 (a British record for a locomotive-operated line). The average speed on the line is 5 mph. Included in the engineering works were two viaducts over the River Hwch, the lower 166 yards long with 14 arches, and the upper 53 yards long with four arches. The whole track was laid in 72 working days (an average of around 120 yards every day) and the first works train reached the summit on 6 January, 1896 – although at this time station buildings were not completed, some fences needed to be erected and the signalling system had yet to be installed.

The official opening on 6 April, 1896, was marred by the only serious incident in the line's history. *Ladas*, the locomotive of the first of two descending trains, disengaged from the rack on the steepest part of the line (possibly because of distortion of the line by frost), gathered speed, came off the track and plunged into Cwm Glas Bach – but not before the driver and fireman had jumped clear. As it left the track, it damaged telegraph poles and cables, resulting in the bell ringing at the summit as the starting signal for the following train. Before the carriages behind *Ladas* were stopped, a passenger jumped out and suffered terrible injuries that proved fatal. The following train collided with the two (now empty) carriages and these were pushed along the line. The line was immediately closed and did not reopen until 1897, by when inverted L-shaped guard rails, known as grippergirders, had been laid on either side of the racks and gripper shoes fitted to the locomotives that would engage the girders and prevent complete derailment. Since then the railway has enjoyed a virtually troublefree history.

The grandeur of Snowdon impresses regardless of the weather, but in wet and cloudy conditions the magnificence of the scenery is blotted out by swirling cloud and the biting wind and dashing rain seem to penetrate the most protective of clothing. When the weather is fine, the views are unmatched in the British Isles. From the base station at Llanberis the line initially climbs at a gentle 1 in 50, rapidly changing to a stiff 1 in 6 accompanied by a roar from the locomotive as it starts the hard ascent. The line crosses the viaducts, passes through Waterfall Halt (with views of the spectacular Ceunant Mawr waterfalls), Hebron Station (1069ft, the first stopping and passing point), Halfway Station (1641ft and where water is taken on), Rocky Valley Halt, Clogwyn Station (2556ft, with a view of the Menai Strait) and on to Summit Station. At the summit there are tourist and refreshment facilities. The original building was first opened in 1898, replacing a number of huts, but the present buildings were erected in 1934 and have been modernized from time to time. The journey takes an hour in each direction.

The Snowdon Mountain Railway has owned eight 0-4-2 steam locomotives, all built by SLM at Winterthur in Switzerland, and details of these are given below. The locomotives were designed to be able to push two coaches and this is how they were used for a few years. Single-carriage operation is, however, now standard. Each locomotive has a handbrake on each of the two driving axles and a governor-controlled steam brake, which is automatically applied if the speed exceeds 7 mph. On the downhill journey the speed is controlled by a system known as 'counter pressure braking', in which the locomotive, in effect, acts as an air compressor. The driver controls the speed by varying the rate at which the compressed air is discharged to the atmosphere. All the steam locomotives have boilers inclined to the frame so that they are approximately level when ascending and descending. Two purpose-built 0-4-0 diesel locomotives were acquired in 1986 and a third is scheduled for delivery in April/May 1991. The original 50-seat carriages with wooden seats and no glazing, built in the main by the Lancaster Railway Carriage and Wagon Co. Ltd., have long been replaced by modern fully glazed coaches. All are bogie coaches and each is fitted with an independent braking system.

Station, on the descent to Llanberis.

diesels delivered in 1986, *Ninian* is seen heading for Hebron, with a steam train in the background. The summit of Snowdon is shrouded in mist.

Ralph, delivered in 1923, steams through Rocky Valley. The main difference from earlier locomotives is the larger water tank that avoids the need to stop for water on the ascent and descent.

Above: A train descends towards Clogwyn Station.

Snowdon at Clogwyn Station. This photograph shows clearly the double-bladed rack system used on the railway.

Photography: Probably the best plan is to ride up in the train and walk back down the footpath to Llanberis, which follows the line closely for part of its route. A narrow and steep road leads up from Llanberis to an overbridge about a mile from Snowdon Station and close to Hebron Station. The only opportunity for photographing the front of a Snowdon locomotive is at the shed at Llanberis. Locomotives on the approach tracks can be photographed from the upper part of the station yard.

Other Attractions: Whilst nothing can match the splendour of Snowdon, both the Llanberis Lake Railway, the National Slate Museum of Wales and the Power of Wales exhibition are nearby.

Services: Trains run every day from 15 March to 1 November. Although the Railway uses its best endeavours to run the 9.30, 11.30 and 13.30 trains every day (provided that there are at least ten passengers), there is not otherwise a strict timetable. The first train is scheduled to leave Llanberis at 9 am (8.30 am during peak periods) and thereafter half-hourly until 1700 hours (15.30 on Saturdays), but trains run frequently according to weather and, provided that there are at least 25 passengers, until mid/late afternoon. In severe weather conditions (normally early and late season) train services terminate at Clogwyn (three-quarters of the way to the summit) or Rocky Valley Halt. For further information telephone 0286-870223 or write to The General Manager, Snowdon Mountain Railway, Llanberis, Gwynedd, LL55 4TY.

Locomotives

No. 1 Ladas (more properly L.A.D.A.S.)

Delivered in 1895, works number 923. Named after Mrs. Laura Alice Duff Assheton Smith, using only her initials for simplicity, the wife of landowner G. W. Duff Assheton Smith, who made available all the land on which the railway was constructed. Was destroyed in the accident on the opening day in 1896.

No. 2 Enid

Named after the daughter of G. W. Duff Assheton Smith. This is the oldest locomotive now working on the line and is the same basic design as Nos. 1, 3, 4 and 5. Delivered in 1895, works number 924. Enid Duff Assheton Smith (as a little girl of 8 years old) cut the first sod on the construction of the line in December 1894.

No. 3 Wyddfa

Delivered in 1895, works number 925. Yr Wyddfa is Welsh for Snowdon.

No. 4 Snowdon

Delivered in 1896, works number 988. Withdrawn from service in 1939. Rebuilt by Hunslet in 1961 and resumed service in 1963.

An early morning works train pushed by *Snowdon* at the summit of the mountain.

No. 5 Moel Siabod

Delivered in late 1897, works number 989. The name is that of one of the mountains in Snowdonia, overlooking Capel Curig.

No. 6 Padarn

Delivered in 1922, works number 2823. Revised design with superheated boilers (compared to the earlier saturated steam locomotives) and the sides of the panniers cut back to expose the lower sides of the boiler. Originally named *Sir Harmood* (Sir John Sutherland Harmood Banner was the first chairman of the Company) and renamed *Padarn* in 1928. The locomotive is dedicated to St. Padarn, an early Christian Saint who lived in the area in the 6th century. Being overhauled at the time of writing.

No. 7 Ralph

Delivered in 1923, works number 2869. Design as for *Padarn*, but with larger water tank, enabling it to ascend and descend without stopping for water. Original name *Aylwin*, changed to *Ralph Sadler* (Company engineer 1964–77) and more recently to *Ralph*.

No. 8 Eryri

Delivered in 1923, works number 2870. Specification as for *Ralph*. Eryri is Welsh for Snowdonia.

No. 9 Ninian

Delivered in 1986, 0-4-0 diesel locomotive with 320hp Rolls-Royce engine built by Hunslet of Leeds, works number 9249. The transmission incorporates a Clark torque converter and downhill speed is controlled by a hydrodynamic brake (with Voith retarder). It is dedicated to Ninian Rhys Davies, Chairman of the Company, and to the Davies family associated with the Railway since 1922.

No. 10 Yeti

Delivered in 1986, identical to No. 9 and with works number 9250. The name was chosen after a competition on BBC TV and the locomotive is dedicated to 'all creatures of the mountains; living and legendary'.

Sir Haydn running as a *West Coast Special* on the Dolgoch Viaduct during the Gala Weekend in 1990.

Talyllyn Railway

The construction of the Talyllyn was prompted by the same commercial reasons as the Ffestiniog, the more economical transport of slate. From the Bryn Eglwys slate quarry, near Abergynolwyn, the slate was carried by pack horse to Aberdovey for shipment. The McConnel family, who owned the quarry, engaged James Winter Spooner (elder brother of Charles Spooner of the Ffestiniog) to survey a line and he proposed an approximately 6½-mile route from Towyn (now Tywyn) to Abergynolwyn, rising steadily and with a three-arch viaduct spanning the deep but narrow gorge of the Dolgoch Falls. It was not a complete solution, for slate would still have to be lowered by three rope-worked inclines to Nant Gwernol and transported from Abergynolwyn by light tramway.

Construction was approved by Private Act of Parliament passed in July 1865 and provided that the gauge should be less than 4ft 8½in and not less than 2ft 3in and that the speed of the trains should be limited to 15 mph. For reasons that are still far from clear, construction of the railway to 2ft 3in gauge had started in April 1864 and was virtually completed by the time that the Act had been passed. As early as September 1864 the first locomotive, an 0-4-0 saddle tank, was delivered by Fletcher Jennings & Co. of Whitehaven and named *Talyllyn*. It was used in the construction of the railway and for slate carrying once the line was open. Because of an excessive rear overhang, it was far from satisfactory. A second locomotive from Fletcher Jennings, an 0-4-0 saddle tank of improved design without the rear overhang, followed in 1866 and was named *Dolgoch*. On its arrival *Talyllyn* was returned to the makers to be rebuilt to 0-4-2 layout.

Passenger services commenced in late 1866 and soon afterwards an intermediate station was opened at Rhydronen. The Talyllyn Railway operated in a very quiet and modest way and in 1911 both the quarry and the railway were bought by Towyn businessman Sir Henry Haydn Jones (who was also for many years the Liberal Member of Parliament for the district). Operation of the railway continued through the years of the Second World War (albeit on a 'skeleton' basis) and still operated after the cease of quarrying at Bryn Eglwys in 1946. By 1947 trains were running only three days a week, both track and rolling stock were almost derelict and trains were frequently late and sometimes did not run at all. The Talyllyn escaped nationalization in 1948, Sir Henry died in 1950 and a group of enthusiasts, headed by author and engineer L. T. C. Rolt, formed the Talyllyn Railway Preservation Society. Agreement was reached in February 1951 whereby Lady Hadyn Jones, widow of Sir Henry, transferred all the shares in the railway company to a holding company and operation passed to the Talyllyn Railway Preservation Society.

The Talyllyn was the pioneer of preservation societies, and by a combination of hard work by the many volunteers of the society, intensive efforts by the few paid staff and a good deal of generous support, the railway was restored to a splendour that exceeded anything seen during its commercial days.

Tywyn Station has been substantially rebuilt and extended in recent years and there is also a new track layout built by the Preservation Society. *Sir Hadyn* **is about to leave with a train.**

The Society's ambition was always to extend the railway a further three-quarters of a mile, over the private mineral tramway to Nant Gwernol, and this was finally accomplished in 1976.

For practical reasons most journeys on the Talyllyn commence at Wharf Station at Tywyn, where there are good parking facilities, both the Society's own, very close to the station, and a Council car park within comfortable walking distance. Wharf Station was originally a slate transhipment yard (the former Cambrian main line runs immediately to the south of the station) with a brick-built booking office. Changes to the track layout were made in 1952 to incorporate a run-round loop and a short platform and in 1960 a carriage siding was laid. In 1964–5 the station was completely redeveloped with new tracks and platform, the Narrow Gauge Railway Museum was extended and the station building was enlarged. Other improvements, including a platform canopy and new booking hall, have followed over the years.

Just over a quarter of a mile up from Towyn is Pendre Station (the original passenger terminus) and Pendre Works, with the Northern Carriage Shed to the left of the line and to the right the Engine Shed and Southern Carriage Shed, which were built in 1867, but which, in recent years, have been refurbished and improved. As the train leaves Pendre it passes the only gated level crossing on the line. It then climbs steadily through farm land to Rhydyronen (just after 2 miles), the hills begin to close in and Brynglas (3¼ miles) is reached. The line now follows a hillside shelf, crosses the Dolgoch ravine over the three-span brick viaduct and enters Dolgoch Station (5 miles). Here water is usual taken on and many passengers leave the train to view the magnificent falls.

No. 6 *Douglas* being watered at Tywyn. This Andrew Barclay-built 0-4-0 was presented to the Talyllyn on the understanding that it was named *Douglas*. It was used infrequently in 1990 because of boiler problems and is now out of service for boiler replacement.

Above: Originally part of the stock of the Corris Railway, No. 3 *Sir Haydn* is just about to pass under the main road bridge at Tywyn.

Left: Dolgoch, one of the original Talyllyn saddle-tank locomotives, delivered in 1865, seen receiving maintenance in the shed at Pendre Works.

Below: Dolgoch and *Peter Sam* (formerly *Edward Thomas*), another ex-Corris Railway locomotive, outside the works at Pendre.

Brynglas Halt, 3¼ miles from Tywyn, with the driver of *Douglas* about to receive the token for the new section of the line.

From Dolgoch the line continues to climb along the hillside shelf, passes through Quarry Siding Halt and runs through high open country with views of the Cader range of mountains. Until 1976 Abergynolwyn (6½ miles) was the upper terminus for passenger trains. The grey stone station building, incorporating refreshment facilities, looks as old as the line, but was only completed in 1969. When the extension to Nant Gwernol was opened, the platform was lengthened so that it can accommodate two trains at once. As the line continues on to Nant Gwernol, so the valley opens up again, with some of the finest views on the railway. A short distance from the station there is a footbridge spanning a narrow gorge and fine views of a spectacular waterfall. The Society, working with the Forestry Commission, has opened a series of forest walks in the area. The trains stop only briefly at Nant Gwernol and return to Abergynolwyn for a longer, refreshment stop before continuing the downhill journey.

The Talyllyn has a much extended stud of locomotives, details of which are given below. Three of the carriages, together with a brake van, were part of the original rolling stock supplied to the railway by Brown Marshalls & Co. of Birmingham. Although fitted with doors on both sides, the Talyllyn has platforms only on the uphill left side, in common with other narrow-gauge railways, and it was a requirement of the Railway Inspectorate that the doors on the non-platform side were permanently fastened before they entered service. In 1952–3 the Talyllyn acquired two four-wheeled carriages that had been used on the Penrhyn Quarry Railway and one of these remains in service. Other carriages incorporate ex-Penrhyn bodies and there are a number of other historic carriages. The railway has also, since 1965, gradually added bogie carriages of new construction but traditional appearance.

The very first locomotive to be delivered to the *Talyllyn* in 1864, No. 1, *Talyllyn*, rebuilt in 1886 as an 0-4-2 to improve stability. It is seen about ¾ of a mile up the line from Brynglas Halt. Note the traditional slate fencing.

Another view of *Talyllyn*, about ¾ of a mile from Dolgoch Falls and about to enter the short wooded section of the line.

Below: Another view of the three-arch brick Dolgoch Viaduct with *Peter Sam* crossing.

Above: **Water is taken on at Dolgoch Station and in this case the locomotive is No. 3, *Sir Haydn*.**

In early Spring 1990 *Sir Haydn* steams through the woods after Dolgoch.

***Talyllyn* about ¾-mile outside Dolgoch. This is one of the few stretches where the photographer's view of the line is unbroken by trees in the foreground and a photograph of the whole train can be taken.**

Dolgoch returning to Tywyn through the Fathew Valley below Dolgoch Falls.

Another view of *Dolgoch*, approaching the wood near Abergynolwyn.

Peter Sam approaching Abergynolwyn.

Photography: The bridge at Wharf Station and Dolgoch Station, where the locomotives take on water, are always favourite vantage points. Likewise the level crossings on the line make excellent spots for photography. However, there is no substitute for careful study of the Ordnance Survey sheet to locate unusual points from which photographs can be taken safely and without trespassing.

Other Attractions: Aberdovey is a pleasant seaside resort and makes a good base from which to visit all the narrow-gauge railways.

Services: Trains operate daily from the beginning of April through to the beginning of November, and from Boxing Day to New Year's Day. For further information telephone 0654-710472 or write to The General Manager, Talyllyn Railway Preservation Society, Wharf Station, Tywyn, Gwynedd.

Above left: **A rare view of** *Douglas* **at Abergynolwyn Station.**

Above: *Peter Sam***'s driver sums up the character of the Talyllyn.**

Right away for *Peter Sam* **at Abergynolwyn as it is about to depart for Nant Gwernol.**

Locomotives

No. 1 Talyllyn   0-4-2 ST

Delivered by Fletcher Jennings & Co of Whitehaven in September 1864 while the railway was still being built. Because of the extended rear overhang, it was rebuilt in 1886 and returned to the railway in 1887 as an 0-4-2. Believed to have had boiler repairs when at Whitehaven some 30 years later and subsequently rebuilt on new steel frames at Pendre. Ceased work in 1945, was rebuilt in 1957, returned to service in 1958, proved a poor steamer and prone to breakdowns, taken out of service in 1968, extensively modified at Pendre, returned to service in 1972. It was withdrawn in 1982 for further modifications and soon back again in service.

No. 2 Dolgoch   0-4-0 ST

Much revised saddle tank built by Fletcher Jennings & Co to avoid the long rear overhang by placing the firebox ahead of the rear axle and delivered in 1865. The only usable engine on the railway between 1946 and 1951. Taken out of service in late 1953 and after many delays returned to service in 1963. Stripped down in 1977, extensively repaired and returned to service in 1980.

No. 3 Sir Haydn/Sir Handel   0-4-0 ST

One of three identical 0-4-0 saddle tanks that formed the original stock of the Corris Railway, it was built by Hughes Locomotive and Tramway Engine Co., Loughborough in 1878. Rebuilt in 1920 by Corris and withdrawn from service on the closure of the railway in 1948. Acquired by the Talyllyn in 1951, entered service that year, but withdrawn because of track problems. Re-entered service in 1953, withdrawn in 1958 and after rebuild returned to service in 1968. In 1982 it was repainted red and temporarily renamed *Sir Handel*, in imitation of the locomotive of the Skarloey railway, featured in the books by the Rev. W. Audrey.

No. 4 Edward Thomas/Peter Sam   0-4-0 ST

Built for the Corris Railway by Kerr Stuart & Co. Ltd, Stoke on Trent in 1921, and withdrawn for boiler repairs in 1947. After initial work at Pendre, overhauled by the Hunslet Engine Co. Ltd at Leeds and re-entered service in 1952. In 1958 it was fitted experimentally with a Giesl Ejector blastpipe and chimney. A new boiler was fitted in 1964, major overhaul in 1976, returned to service in 1978. Since 1988 the locomotive has been painted red and temporarily named *Peter Sam*, in imitation of the locomotive of the Skarloey railway, featured in the books by Rev. W. Audrey.

No. 6 Douglas   0-4-0 T

Constructed by Andrew Barclay Sons & Co. Ltd, Kilmarnock, in 1918 to 2ft gauge and given to the Talyllyn in 1953 by Abelson & Co (Engineers) Ltd on the understanding that it should be named *Douglas* after Mr. Douglas Abelson. From 1921 to 1945 it had operated at RAF Calshot. After overhaul and conversion to 2ft 3in gauge, entered service in 1954.

No. 7	0-4-2 T

Built by Andrew Barclay in 1948 to 3ft gauge and supplied to Bord na Mona (the Irish Turf Board) for hauling turf fuel to power stations. Was also turf-burning. Purchased by the Talyllyn 1969 to form the basis of a new locomotive to be built at Pendre. Construction commenced in 1971, but only limited progress made following a decline in traffic from 1973 onwards.

**Talyllyn comes off the loop at Nant Gwernol to join
up with the train for the descent to Tywyn.**

Diesel Locomotives

No. 5 Midlander	0-4-0

Built by Ruston Hornsby to 2ft 6½in gauge in 1940 for Jee's Hartshill Quarries, Nuneaton, and operated until 1956. Acquired by the Talyllyn and delivered with gauge modified to 2ft 3in in 1957. After 1976 went into store and returned to service in 1980 with the engine, transmission and superstructure from another locomotive of the same type.

No. 8 Merseysider	0-4-0

One of two locomotives with hydrostatic drive built by Ruston to 3ft gauge in 1964 for Park Gate Steel Works, Rotherham. After closure of the works both were acquired by the Talyllyn in 1969, and No. 8 represents a re-gauged composite of the two.

No. 9 Alf	0-4-0

Built by Hunslet Engine Co. in 1950 for the National Coal Board and was one of two acquired by the Talyllyn in 1970. This locomotive was overhauled and put into service and the other is used for spares. Primarily suited for heavy haulage.

Alan George, being meticulously oiled.

Teifi Valley Railway

Today's Teifi Valley is built on the trackbed of part of the Carmarthen and Cardigan Railway, intended to link the broad gauge South Wales Railway at Carmarthen with the port of Cardigan. By 1864 the line had reached Llandysul, the South Wales Railway was absorbed by the Great Western, in 1872 the railway was converted to standard gauge and the Carmarthen and Cardigan had no alternative but to follow. The Carmarthen and Cardigan was itself taken over by the Great Western in 1881 and although the line was extended to Newcastle Emlyn in 1895, it never reached Cardigan. Passenger services ceased on the Newcastle Emlyn branch on 15 September, 1952 and the line was finally closed to freight on 28 September, 1975. The rails were removed and the buildings were demolished, although a tunnel and bridges remained.

In August 1978 the Vale of Teifi Narrow Gauge Railway Society was formed and in January, 1981 the trackbed between Pencader Junction and Newcastle Emlyn was acquired from British Rail, but the three miles from Pencader Junction to Llandysul was sold in 1988, as it was surplus to requirements. The Dyfed Railway Company Limited was formed to own the track and operate the railway. Work on construction of the 2ft-gauge railway began in the autumn of 1983, with the support of the Manpower Services Commission, with initially the first mile from Henllan constructed, together with a new toilet block and resurfaced car park at Henllan. A children's playground, garden areas, a mile-long Nature Trail and an open air Theatre in the woods were also created. In addition two wooden buildings were erected by members of the Society as shop/ticket office and refreshment rooms. The first mile to Pontprenshitw opened in 1986, the line now runs for a little over 1¼ miles and in November 1988 the operating company became known as The Teifi Valley Railway plc.

From Henllan the line runs through Forest Halt, used by passengers wanting to visit the open air theatre or take the woodland walks, across the stone-built bridge over the River Cynllo at Pontprenshitw ('shaky wooden bridge' and referring to the original which was replaced in 1893) and terminates at Llandyfriog.

The mainstay of the Teifi is *Alan George*, a small 0-4-0 saddle tank built by Hunslet, works number 606, in 1894 for the Penrhyn Slate Quarries. It was purchased by a syndicate of Railway Society members. The railway also has *Sholto*, a Hudson Hunslet 0-4-0 diesel, works number 2433, built in 1931 and a 1959 Simplex diesel, works number 11111, named *Sammy*. There are four passenger coaches, all with wooden bodies constructed at Henllan, three on underframes acquired from Trentham Gardens and one completed in 1990 on an underframe constructed in 1988 at the Talyllyn Railway.

Photography: There are no photographic problems and the full length of the line is suitable for photography.

Alan George, **one of the quaintest locomotives on Welsh narrow-gauge railways and the mainstay of locomotive power on the Teifi.**

Other Attractions: These include the Henllan Falls, Velingeri, a restored flour mill outside Newcastle Emlyn and the Woollen Mill Museum for Wales at Velindre. Both the Vale of Rheidol and Gwili Railways are nearby.

Services: The railway operates every day from Good Friday until October and trains depart hourly from 11am to 6pm. In addition 'Santa Specials' operate just before Christmas. For further information telephone 0559-371077 or write to the Teifi Valley Railway plc, Station Yard, Henllan, Llandysul, Dyfed.

Through the conifers at Gwaith-coch (red workings) scree *Llywelyn* heads towards Devil's Bridge

Vale of Rheidol Light Railway

Construction of the Vale of Rheidol was encouraged in the 1890s by the commercial prospects of linking the blossoming seaside resort of Aberystwyth with the beauty spot of Devil's Bridge, a distance of 11¾ miles to the east. In addition there was the prospect of mining traffic, mainly lead ore, from the Ystwyth Valley to feed the foundries of Aberystwyth. At an early stage a standard-gauge (4ft 8½in) line was rejected because of the high cost of running the line along a shelf cut in the steep sides of the Rheidol gorge. The Vale of Rheidol (Light) Railway Act was passed in August 1897, authorizing the construction of a 2ft-gauge railway (in reality 1ft 11½in) and a public subscription was raised. It was not until January 1901 that a contract for the construction of the line was placed and completion of the line to Devil's Bridge was accomplished on 28 July, 1902.

Initially the line was opened in August for goods traffic only, because Major Druitt of the Railway Inspectorate objected to the sharp curvature of several parts of the line and unconsolidated track. Commercial traffic made a good start and regular passenger services commenced on 22 December, 1902. Initially there were stations at Aberystwyth, Llanbadarn, Capel Bangor, Nant-y-ronen, Aberffrwd and Devil's Bridge, and additional halts were added at Rheidol Falls (from 7 March, 1904) and Glanrafon Halt (7 May, 1904). A goods branch to Stone Quay, Aberystwyth, was opened in 1902, but this was soon to all intents and purposes abandoned and the rails were lifted in about 1930.

Llywelyn, **painted in Cambrian Railway livery, outside the shed that was used formerly for standard-gauge main-line locomotives.**

Owain Glyndŵr pulling out of Aberystwyth Station. All locomotives on the Vale of Rheidol are now oil-fired.

The level crossing at Llanbadarn. Sophisticated level crossing warnings have been installed because of accidents in the past.

Below: Llywelyn on the timber viaduct over the River Rheidol, which is scheduled for rebuilding.

On 1 August, 1913, the Cambrian Railway took control of the line, at a time when it was at its peak of popularity. During the First World War the service deteriorated, partly because of the decline of the mines that used the line, the timetable was much reduced and the railway was even closed for periods of months. The Great Western Railway took over the Cambrian on 1 January, 1923, as part of the railway groupings. Efforts were made to revitalize the line and two new locomotives, based on the original design, and four bogie observation carriages were built at Swindon in 1923, and a third new locomotive, albeit said to be a rebuild, followed in 1924. In 1925 the Aberystwyth terminus was moved to a new site alongside the main-line station. By this stage the mines traffic was affected by road transport opposition and goods operations ceased on 1 January, 1927. From the beginning of 1931 regular passenger services, undermined by 'charabanc' services, also ceased, and the Rheidol became a purely tourist line, without a winter schedule. In 1938 new observation coaches replaced the existing rolling stock. By 1940 work was completed on a new 210ft-long engine shed to replace the original 150ft Cambrian shed, and here the locomotives were stored during the war years while services were suspended. Services started again on 23 July, 1945, and on nationalization in 1948 the line became part of British Railways.

For some years the Vale of Rheidol ran steadily, unspectactularly and in continuing decline, although the stock was smartened up in 1954 by repainting the locomotives in Western Region express green and the carriages in a variant of GWR chocolate and cream. Although there was talk of closure, this was accompanied by a reawakening of interest in Welsh narrow-gauge railways and the line carried on. In

Owain Glyndŵr **on the level crossing at Nant-y-ronen Halt. Here the locomotive takes on water, but it is planned that taking on water will be transferred to Aberffrwd.**

At a point about nine miles from Aberystwyth *Llywelyn* approaches Rheidol Falls. Just down the line towards Devil's Bridge there is a commemorative stone to Oliver Veltom, a senior railwayman on the line whose ashes were scattered nearby.

Owain Glyndŵr at Gwaith-coch with the superb landscape of the Rheidol Valley in the background. This is the only point on the line with such a good view of the valley, but extensive tree pruning is planned.

Another view of *Owain Glyndŵr* at the sharp curve after Gwaith-coch, 9¼ miles from Aberystwyth. Here the line turns towards Cwm Rhiw-Gos, a valley for which there is no equivalent name in English.

1956 the three locomotives were named, No. 7, *Owain Glyndŵr* No. 8, *Llywelyn* and No. 9, *Prince of Wales,* and a year later they were repainted in Brunswick green lined out in black and orange. There was a small, but steady increase in traffic and in 1963, as part of a major reorganization, the line was transferred to the London Midland Region of British Rail. All intermediate halts were closed, the Rheidol took over the standard-gauge locomotive shed at Aberystwyth following its closure in 1965 and by 1968 the line had been re-routed over the track-bed of the former Carmarthen line, past its newly acquired engine shed and into the former Carmarthen bays at the main station.

Because of the fire hazards in the forested areas through which the line runs, and the high cost of forestry patrols incurred during the hot summer of 1976, *Owain Glyndŵr* was converted to oil firing by the start of the 1978 season, and the other two locomotives were subsequently converted. That same year a rather ugly temporary building was erected at Devil's Bridge to act as a buffet. Extra Portacabin facilities were provided in 1989. There were many plans for the privatization of the line, which has been supported since 1970 by the Vale of Rheidol Supporters Association, but these came to nothing until a final decision to sell was made in 1987. The Vale of Rheidol was bought in 1989 by the owners of the Brecon Mountain Railway, who are implementing a programme of steady improvement and development, including replacing much of the trackwork, upgrading level crossings and providing additional facilities. In the long term new buildings are planned at both Aberystwyth and Devil's Bridge.

Llywelyn heading through the woods towards Devil's Bridge.

Owain Glyndŵr, at Devil's Bridge Station.

Overhead view of *Owain Glyndŵr* from the Dorman Long
bridge, the only overbridge on the line, just before

Owain Glyndŵr at Quarry Cutting on the approach to Devil's Bridge.

Another view of *Owain Glyndŵr* at Devil's Bridge Station.

The Vale of Rheidol is one of the most scenic of the Welsh narrow-gauge railways. From the Aberystwyth terminus the line runs parallel to the standard-gauge for 1½ miles until Llanbadarn Station is reached, where the main line veers to the north, crosses a very minor road and then reaches the River Rheidol, crossed by a timber viaduct. Next comes Glanrafon Halt (2¾ miles) as the railway follows the valley bottom, then Capel Bangor, across another ungated level crossing, soon followed by a stiff climb, with a short stretch of 1 in 50. Now the line twists and turns along a shelf on the hillside, through woods and cuttings with superb views of the Rheidol Valley. Sometimes the views are but a mere glimpse, and extensive pruning of the trees would do much to enhance the splendid view.

Next comes Nant-y-ronen Halt (6½ miles), once a real station, and then Aberffrwd, for many years the main intermediate station. A passing loop was installed in 1990 to replace that taken up by BR in the 1960s. Now that Aberffrwd is re-established as a passing place, with most trains booked to stop, it is expected that many passengers will want to disembark for a few minutes. The watering facilities are to be reinstated and once these are working satisfactorily, the tank at Nant-y-ronen, where mid-way watering takes place at the present time, will be transferred to Aberystwyth to replace the old standard-gauge tank, which will soon need major work. From Aberffrwd to Devil's Bridge the locomotive faces a stiff climb, 1 in 50 for most of the way. From here onwards the views across the valley are at their best, despite the dam and buildings of Cwm Rheidol hydroelectricity scheme and lake stretching along the valley. After Rheidol Falls Halt the train passes the derelict Caegynon mine, reaches Rhiwfron (10¾ miles) and steams under the overbridge into Devil's Bridge station.

Locomotive power is provided by the magnificent stud of three 2-6-2s, more fully described below. In addition there is diesel No. 10, used for works trains, shunting and emergency cover .

Photography: For much of the line photography is difficult, but some of the photographs shown here give an indication of the possibilities. The level crossing at Capel Bangor is easily reached by car, as are the halts at Aberffrwd and Nant-y-ronen. Another good spot is the overbridge at Devil's Bridge.

Other Attractions: The line links the main attractions in the local areas, Aberystwyth and Devil's Bridge. The latter consists of three bridges, the lowest of which is believed to have been erected by the monks of Strata Florida Abbey in 1087 and is the 'Devil's Bridge', with the upper bridges erected in 1753 and 1901. Under the bridges is the foaming whirlpool known as the Devil's Punchbowl and a series of waterfalls. They are within a few hundred yards of the station.

Services: Operates daily from Easter to the end of September. All trains finish the day at Aberystwyth, so it is not possible to make a round trip from Devil's Bridge with a late departure. There is excellent parking at both Aberystwyth and Devil's Bridge. For further information telephone 0685-4854 or write to the General Manager, c/o Brecon Mountain Railway, Pant Station, Merthyr Tydfil, Mid Glamorgan, CF48 2UP.

Locomotives

No. 7 Owain Glyndŵr   2-6-2 T

Swindon-built in 1923, following the original design of the Davis & Metcalfe 2-6-2s ordered for the opening of the line. These were substantial locomotives with outside frames and cylinders, full-length tanks and Stephenson valve gear inside the frames and in front of the driving wheels. The Swindon version was based on the same drawings, but was slightly heavier, slightly more powerful, with outside frames and outside Walschaerts' valve gear. *Owain Glyndŵr* was originally painted Great Western locomotive green and was not named until 1956. It was painted British Rail blue in 1968 and converted to oil burning in 1978. Repainted present Western Region green in 1983. Received major boiler repairs over the winter of 1990–91.

No. 8 Llywelyn   2-6-2 T

Swindon-built in 1923, following the original design of Davis & Metcalfe 2-6-2s (see above). Originally painted plain unlined Great Western locomotive green, and not named until 1956. Painted British Rail blue in 1968 and converted to oil-burning in 1979. In 1980 the name-plate was removed in accordance with Cambrian Railway practice, the locomotive was repainted Cambrian black (which has just a hint of green) with that railway's name, CAMBRIAN, in 7in letters extending 6ft along the tank sides. The letters and numbers are Cambrian's French grey, with the letters shaded red to the right and below, and there are red buffer beams. Scheduled for a full rebuild starting in late 1991.

No. 9 Prince of Wales   2-6-2 T

The two Davis & Metcalfe tank engines survived on the line into the takeover by the Great Western. No. 1, *Edward VII*, became No. 1212 under the GWR reign and was withdrawn after the cessation of winter passenger services in 1931, dispatched to Swindon in 1932 and scrapped in 1935. No. 2, *Prince of Wales*, renumbered No. 1213, had been sent to Swindon for overhaul in 1924, but what emerged was a completely new locomotive, very similar to Nos. 7 and 8. Painted unlined Great Western green. Painted black and renumbered No. 9 under British Rail, repainted green and named in 1956. Repainted British Rail blue in 1967, converted to oil-burning in 1981 and repainted as close as possible to the original 1902 Vale of Rheidol olive green and claret colours. After major overhaul at the Brecon Mountain Railway, scheduled to re-enter service in 1991 painted deep crimson.

Russell, one of the most famous of all Welsh narrow-gauge locomotives, pulling out of Porthmadog Station whilst on loan to the Ffestiniog.

Welsh Highland Railway

The Welsh Highland is a railway with a magnificent past, a modest but ambitious present and massive potential. The original Welsh Highland Railway with a gauge of 2ft was formed as late as 1922 by the merger of the North Wales Narrow Gauge Railway, opened in 1877, running from Dinas near Caernarfon to Rhyd-ddu (after it had been extended in 1881) and combining the carriage of passengers, slate, general and agricultural traffic with the Croesor Tramway, a horse-worked line opened in 1860 and carrying slate from the Croesor Valley to Porthmadog for shipping. With a length of 22 miles the Welsh Highland was the longest narrow-gauge Welsh railway and its route was the most spectacular, taking in the Pass of Aberglaslyn, the very attractive village of Beddgelert and the southern slopes of Snowdon itself.

Another view of *Russell*, on the Welsh Highland. To the left is the main shed.

***Karen*, built in 1942 for operation in what was then Southern Rhodesia, was moved to the Welsh Highland in 1976 and entered service in 1983.**

It was not unfortunately a commercial success and as the demand for slate diminished, so the railway died. The line closed in 1937, in 1940 the stock was sold off, the rails were lifted in 1941 and since 1942 the track-bed has been in the hands of a liquidator and latterly the Official Receiver. In 1961 the Welsh Highland Railway Society was formed and three years later it became The Welsh Highland Light Railway (1964) Limited. Determined to restore the line to its former glory, in 1976 the new company purchased from British Rail the old slate exchange siding at Porthmadog known as Beddgelert Sidings and adjacent to the old Welsh Highland line. This was followed a year later by the purchase of land known as Gelert's Farm, lying in the triangle between the old track-bed, Beddgelert Sidings and the British Rail Cambrian Coast main line. The company relaid the track, purchased locomotives and constructed coaches. By 1980 the new Welsh Highland was operating over three-quarters of a mile of restored track between Porthmadog and Pen-y-Mount.

The plans remained bold and forward-looking. The next step is to extend the 1½ miles to the river crossing at Pont Croesor, and rejoin the original track-bed. Negotiations between the Welsh Highland Railway (1964) Limited and Gwynedd County Council (itself a creditor of the old Welsh Highland Railway) led to the proposal that the Council should acquire the track-bed of the whole line from the Official Receiver and lease it to the new company in stages. The completion of such a scheme would make Porthmadog the hub of narrow-gauge railways in Wales. In 1987 the Official Receiver received an anonymous bid for the track-bed and it became known in 1990 that the bidder was the Ffestiniog Railway. The Official Receiver applied to the High Court for directions as to the disposal of the track-bed and at the time of writing the Court's decision is still awaited.

The Welsh Highland has a particularly fine stud of locomotives, including the famous *Russell* that ran on the Welsh Highland from 1922 to its closure and has been loaned to the Ffestiniog Railway on a number of occasions. The rolling stock includes two ex-West Highland coaches dating from 1893 and 1907, both of which are to be fully restored. The remainder of the coaches consist of a Passenger Brake built by members that entered service in 1980, two semi-open 'Toastrack' vehicles constructed in the Gelert's Farm works, an ex-Vale of Rheidol brake van dating back to 1902 (but rebuilt in 1938) and an ex-Deutsche Reichsbahn saloon built in 1913.

Photography: Not difficult, but a little uninspiring because of the present shortness of the line. Photographs can be taken at Porthmadog, Pen-y-Mount or in the locomotive shed at which the train stops on its return journey.

Other Attractions: Attractions in the Porthmadog area are numerous, including the Ffestiniog railway, the Porthmadog Maritime Museum, Porthmadog harbour and the Italianate village of Portmeirion.

Services: The Railway is open from Easter to the End of October. It is essential to rely on the timetable published by The Great Little Trains of Wales consortium or to enquire of the Railway. Telephone 0766-513402 (if no reply, then telephone 051-603-2696) or write to the Welsh Highland Railway, Gelert's Farm Works, Madoc Street West, Porthmadog, Gwynedd, LL49 9DY.

Locomotives

Karen	**0-4-2**

Built by Peckett, works number 2024, in 1942 for the Selukwe – Peak Light Railway in the Eastern Highlands of Southern Rhodesia (now Zimbabwe) and placed in store in the late 1950s. Purchased by the Hon. W. McAlpine, shipped to the United Kingdom, sold to a group of Welsh Highland Railway members and moved to Porthmadog early in 1976. Fully restored and entered service in 1983.

Russell	**2-6-2**

Built by Hunslet, works number 901, for the Porthmadog, Beddgelert and South Snowdon Railway in 1906 and transferred to the Welsh Highland Railway on its formation in 1922. Abandoned after the closure of the line and rescued by Birmingham Locomotive Club in 1955. Acquired by the Welsh Highland Light Railway (1964) Limited, completely restored and entered service on Easter Saturday, 1987. Originally ran in 'works grey' livery and finished in the current 'plum' over the winter of 1987–8. In early 1987 she carried the original name plate on loan from the National Railway Museum, but now carries reproductions.

Pedemoura	**0-6-0**

Built by Orenstein & Koppel (Germany) in 1924, works number 10808, for the Minas de Pejao coal mines at Pedorido in Portugal. Imported into the UK by Pleasurerail Limited and acquired by the WHR in 1975. Failed boiler test in 1990. Out of service, awaiting recommendations from the Engineering Department.

Moel Tryfan	**0-4-2**

Built by Bagnall in 1948, works number 2875, for the Rustenberg Platinum Mines in South Africa. Imported 1982, awaiting restoration.

	0-4-2

Built by Bagnall in 1953, works number 3050, for the Rustenberg Platinum Mines in South Africa. Imported 1982, awaiting restoration.

In addition the WHR has a good stud of diesel locomotives which can be summarized as follows:

Glaslyn

Ruston & Hornsby diesel mechanical built 1952, works number 297030, previously owned by Blockleys Ltd of Hadley, loaned to the Llanberis Lake Railway in the 1970s, when known as *Yr Enfys* (The Rainbow). Returned to Porthmadog in 1980 and renamed *Glaslyn*.

Kinnerley

Ruston & Hornsby diesel mechanical built 1953, works number 354068, previously owned by Blockleys Ltd of Hadley.

Cricht

Motor Rail Simplex class diesel mechanical (cabless), built 1941, works number 8703, previously owned by Yorkshire Water Authority and acquired in 1980.

In addition the Railway owns three Motor Rail Simplex class 60hp diesel-mechanicals, previously operated by Pilkingtons on sand excavation works at Rainford, Lancashire. These are Pilkington Nos. 4 (built 1959), 6 (built 1968) and 9 (built 1968), restored and named *Katherine*.

Two Ruston & Hornsby 30hp diesel-mechanicals built 1938 and 1946 and acquired from DSF Refractories (brickworks) await restoration.

Welshpool & Llanfair Light Railway

Opened in 1903, this 2ft 6in-gauge railway linked the market centre of Llanfair Caereinon with the standard-gauge main line at Welshpool, a distance of 9 miles. Although it was owned by the independent Welshpool & Llanfair Light Railway Company, it was operated by the Cambrian Railway, and it was never profitable. Ownership passed to the Great Western Railway on 1 January, 1923, but passenger business was undermined by the GWR's own bus service from Welshpool through Llanfair that started in late 1925 and passenger services ceased on 7 February, 1931. The line remained open for freight only and it was to become the last British non-preserved narrow-gauge railway to carry public freight traffic. In the face of opposition from road traffic, freight fell to low levels and the line was eventually closed on 31 October, 1956.

The month that the railway closed a preservation society was formed and this was replaced by the Welshpool and Llanfair Light Railway Preservation Co. Ltd in 1960. Re-opening of the line between the present Raven Square Terminus and Welshpool British Rail station was not possible because this section had been acquired by the local authority for the building of car parks and a by-pass, although the by-pass plan has now been dropped. The new company used this stretch of the line for works trains for a while, but the track was lifted in August 1963. With a lease of the remainder of the line, the Preservation Company based their operations at Llanfair Caereinion, the first section of 4¼ miles to Castle Caereinon opened in 1963, followed by a further 1¼ miles to Sylfaen in 1964. In December 1964 floods severely damaged the bridge over the River Banwy, and while repairs were undertaken with help from the army, a short shuttle service only operated. By August 1965 services had been resumed as far as Castle Caereinion, but because of extensive work needed to the line, it was not re-opened to Sylfaen until 1972. The freehold of the line was acquired in 1974 and after very extensive works the new terminus at Raven Square was opened in 1981.

Raven Square Station consists at the present time of only a platform and signal box, but by the summer of 1991 a Victorian wooden station from Eardisley, Herefordshire, should have been erected. From the station the train faces a stiff climb, but the track eases as it approaches the open level crossing with New Drive. The line now swings north away from the main A458 road, climbs the steep Golfa incline with nearly a mile at 1 in 29, curves through the trees and runs high on the bank above the Sylfaen Brook. As the railway climbs through the Powis estate, there are magnificent woodland views. After Golfa siding, the line winds its way back towards the A458 and descends to Sylfaen Halt alongside the road. After a stretch of open countryside, the line climbs sharply again, crosses the open level crossing at Coppice Lane and descends through a cutting to Castle Caereinion station. The station has parking facilities and is a good site for a picnic, with superb views to the north-west towards the Berwyn and Arran mountains.

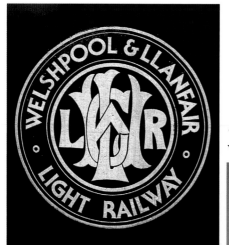

The Countess, one of two 0-6-0 tank locomotives built for the Welshpool in 1902, pulls out of Raven Square Station.

Another photograph taken at Raven Square. This is the 0-8-0 tank locomotive *Sir Drefaldwyn* built in France in 1944 and originally a tender locomotive.

The Countess at Golfa level crossing. The photograph was taken with a Rollei 6006.

As the line leaves the station, a gated level crossing is crossed and the long ascent of Dolarddyn bank, with half a mile at 1 in 32, begins. There is another ungated level crossing at Dolarddyn, followed by a gentle descent to Cyfronydd station. After another level crossing the line curves on to the six-arch Brynelin viaduct, descends at 1 in 24 for a short distance and then follows the River Banwy, crosses the river over a three-span girder viaduct, passes Heniarth Halt and into Llanfair Station. Here there is a buffet and the Preservation Company has erected a two-road locomotive shed and workshop.

The Welshpool and Llanfair has a particularly fine stud of locomotives, including some of truly massive appearance. Five bogie coaches acquired for the reopening of the line in 1963 from the Admiralty (which had used them on the Chattendon and Upnor Railway in Kent) were sold in 1978. There are five end-balcony four-wheeled vehicles built in 1900–1 for the Zillertalbahn in the Austrian Tyrol and there are four bogie saloon coaches built in 1961 for Sierra Leone Railways.

Photography: Because so much of the line runs through open countryside photography is not difficult. There is also plenty of scope at level crossings and at Castle Caereinion Station in particular. The end of the platform at Llanfair, just opposite the sheds, also gives scope for some fascinating photographs.

Other Attractions: Powis Castle is nearby and the Shropshire Union Canal at Welshpool is well worth a visit.

Services: Trains operate at weekends from Easter until October and in December. Daily services are run in the summer holiday months. For further information telephone 0938-810441 or write to The General Manager, The Station, Llanfair Caereinion, Welshpool, Powys, SY21 OSF.

Sir Drefaldwyn **in the woods between Golfa and Sylfaen. An exciting, atmospheric photograph, but locations like this can be found with careful planning, coupled with patience.**

The Welshpool & Llanfair is remarkable for the number of level crossings. This is *Joan*, an 0-6-2 tank locomotive that formerly worked in Antigua, at Coppice Lane Crossing.

Below: The Countess at Castle Caereinion with the last train of the day. The photograph was taken in Spring.

Above: Sir Drefaldwyn at the level crossing after Castle Caereinion.

Hunslet diesel 0-4-0 No. 11 and *Sir Drefaldwyn* at the terminus at Castle Caereinion.

No. 8 *Dougal*, a yard shunter, formerly of Glasgow Corporation's Provan Gasworks and *Joan* at Castle Caereinion. On the right is the locomotive shed and workshop built by the Preservation Company.

Steam Locomotives

No. 2 The Countess   0-6-0 T

Both No. 2 and No. 1, *The Earl* (which was taken out of service for display elsewhere in 1979), were built by Beyer, Peacock & Co. Ltd, Manchester, for the Welshpool and Llanfair in 1902 and alone operated the line until 1956. Both were re-boilered by the GWR in 1929/30, very much in accordance with Swindon practice. *The Countess*, Works Number 3496, operated the line when it was reopened, was withdrawn for overhaul in 1970 and entered service again in 1985.

No. 6 Monarch   0-4-4-0 T

Built in 1953 by W. G. Bagnall Ltd, Stafford. Works Number 3024, it was the last steam narrow-gauge locomotive built for industrial service in Britain. It was supplied new to Bowaters Pulp and Paper Mills at Sittingbourne in Kent and acquired by the Welshpool and Llanfair in 1966. Entered service after major overhaul, but it has not proved as effective as had been hoped and is rarely operated.

No. 8 Dougal   0-4-0 T

Built by Andrew Barclay Sons & Co. Ltd, Kilmarnock, in 1946, Works Number 2207, for Glasgow Corporation's Provan Gasworks. Compact locomotive because of the operating limitations of the Gasworks. Acquired in 1967 and used as a yard shunter.

No. 10 Sir Drefaldwyn   0-8-0T

Built by Société Franco-Belge, Raisme, France, in 1944, Works Number 2855, for the German Military Field Railways and transferred to Austria after the war. Rebuilt by the Styrian Local Government Railways (Steiermarkische Landesbahnen), near Groz from tender to tank engine. Acquired by the Welshpool and Llanfair in 1969.

No. 12 Joan   0-6-2 T

Built by Kerr, Stuart & Co. Ltd, Stoke-on-Trent, in 1927, Works Number 4404, and delivered to Antigua, West Indies to haul sugar cane. Originally equipped for oil-burning, it was converted to coal and sugar cane waste-burning during World War II. Acquired in 1971, overhauled and entered service in 1977.

No. 14   2-6-2 T

Built by the Hunslet Engine Co. Ltd, Leeds, in 1954, Works Number 3815, for Sierra Leone Railways. Acquired in 1975.

The Countess at Llanfair Caereinion.

The Countess undergoing
maintenance in the shed at
Llanfair Caereinion.

No. 15	2-6-2 T

Built by Les Ateliers Metallurgiques, Nivelles, Belgium, Works Number 2369, in 1948 for Jokioisten Railway. On closure of the line in 1972 it was imported into the UK. Moved to Llanfair in 1983, and displayed in yard pending overhaul for service.

Deisel Locomotives

No. 7 Chattenden	0-6-0

Built by E. E. Baguley Ltd, Burton-on-Trent, in 1949. Gardner 150 hp engine. Operated on the Admiralty Upnor and Lodge Hill Railway. Acquired in 1968.

No. 11	0-4-0

Built by the Hunslet Engine Co. Ltd, Leeds, Works Number 2251, in 1941 for the Admiralty. Gardner 50hp engine. Acquired in 1971.

Olwen passing under the road bridge before Llwyfan Cerrig.

Gwili Railway

Preserved railways in South Wales are less than common and the Gwili has a complicated history. In 1854 the Carmarthen & Cardigan Railway was promoted to link Carmarthen with Cardigan, where it was proposed to develop a deep-water port. The line was built to Isambard Kingdom Brunel's (and the Great Western Railway's) 7ft broad gauge. The 18 miles from Carmarthen to Llandysul were completed in June 1864, when the company went into receivership, although the Receiver allowed the railway to continue operations. Just over two years later the Manchester & Milford Railway, notorious for its ambitions and poor finances, was granted running rights over the line, with a third rail to accommodate standard-gauge trains, and a year later the M&M had completed its line through to Aberystwyth. Three years later the M&M was in receivership, the Carmarthen & Cardigan was obliged to switch to 4ft 8½in standard gauge following the Great Western's decision in 1872 to abandon the broad gauge and in 1881 it was absorbed by the Great Western.

The line flourished, mainly with goods traffic, for many years, but the line's fate was sealed when it was severed by serious flooding at Llanilar, about 6 miles south of Aberystwyth on 14 December, 1964, and the last passenger train ran on 20 February, 1965. The last goods service operated in September 1973. A preservation society had been formed in 1972, but this foundered because of lack of support.

Olwen on the first open stretch after Bronwydd Arms. The photograph was taken with a Fujica 6x7.

Olwen **pulls a train across the bridge just before Llwynfan Cerrig Station.**

The Gwili Railway Company was incorporated on 21 April, 1975, and during the summer of that year British Rail began to lift the track. The new company purchased 1¼ miles of track from Bronwydd Arms northwards and later acquired the track-bed for the 8 miles between Abergwili Junction and Llanpumpsaint, including the sites of the stations at Bronwydd Arms and Conwil. Originally the new company operated services from Bronwydd Arms to a new halt at Cwmdwyfran, but now extends 1.6 miles, terminating at Llwyfan Cerrig. An extension to Conwil Station is now being built. The line closely follows the River Gwili, with superb scenery, and the Company has built up a good stud of locomotives. In addition 'guest' locomotives visit the line from time to time.

Photography: The line is set in hilly but open countryside, so photography is not difficult.

Other Attractions: Both Carmarthen Bay and Cardigan Bay are within easy motoring distance.

Services: Telephone 0267-230666 or write to the General Manager, The Gwili Railway, Bronwydd Arms Station, Bronwydd, Carmarthen, Dyfed, SA33 6HT.

Locomotives

Olwen	**0-4-0 ST**

Built by Robert Stephenson & Hawthorn, Newcastle upon Tyne, Works No 7058 in 1942 for Earley Power Station, Reading, where it worked until November 1976. Purchased by the Gwili Railway Preservation Society in 1978 and entered service after protracted overhaul in March 1986.

No. 71516	**0-6-0 ST**

Built by Robert Stephenson & Hawthorn, Newcastle upon Tyne, Works No. 7170, in 1944 for the War Department (one of 484 built to the design by the Hunslet Engine Co. Ltd). In 1947 it was bought by the National Coal Board, working in Northumberland initially, but later transferred to Cynheidre Colliery, Llanelli. On loan to the Gwili Railway Preservative Society from the Welsh Industrial and Maritime Museum and incorporates parts from other locomotives. It is expected to enter service in late 1991 or early in 1992.

No. 1	**0-6-0 ST**

Built by Hudswell Clarke & Co. Leeds, Works No. 1885, in 1955 for the National Coal Board. It worked at Lady Windsor Colliery, Ynysybwl, until 1967, and was taken out of service until 1978. It was donated by the National Coal Board to the Welsh Industrial and Maritime Museum. In 1980 it was loaned on a permanent basis to the Gwili Railway, but it remains in store pending eventual restoration.

Rosyth No. 1	**0-4-0 ST**

Built by Andrew Barclay Sons & Co. Ltd., Kilmarnock, Works Number 1385, in 1914 for the Royal Navy and operated at Rosyth Naval Dockyard, Fife. In 1916 it was transferred to the Royal Air Force, Pembroke Dock, but after a major overhaul in 1955 at Kilmarnock it operated at RAF St. Athan, South Glamorgan, hauling coal. It was withdrawn in 1971 and in 1973 it was acquired by the Railway Club of Wales. It entered service on the Gwili Railway in 1987, and will be available for passenger work from 1991.

Swansea Vale No. 1	**0-4-0 T**

One of a very successful line of four-wheeled geared tank locomotives, with vertical water tube boiler and vertical cylinders inside the body and with chain drive to the wheels built by Sentinel Limited of Shrewsbury. This locomotive, Works Number 9622, was built in 1958 for the Imperial Smelting Corporation Works, Llansamlet. It is the last surviving 200hp Sentinel locomotive of its type. Purchased by the Railway Club of Wales, it was stored at Penderyn Quarry near Hirwaun, later removed to Swansea and went to the Gwili Railway ln 1987.

Deisel Locomotives

Nellie	**0-4-0 Diesel-Electric**

Built ln 1960 by the Yorkshire Engine Co., Sheffield, Works Number 2779, for the Whitehead Steelworks, Newport, Gwent, where it worked until the late 1970s. After some years of storage it was sold to the Gwili Railway Company in August 1982.

Trecatty	**0-6-0 Diesel Mechanical**

Built in 1959 by Ruston and Hornsby, Lincoln, Works Number 421702, for Taylor Woodrow's Royal Arms and Trecatty opencast mines, where it operated until June 1986. It was given to the Gwili Railway Preservation Society by Taylor Woodrow in 1986. It was used on the extension of the line to Llwyfan Cerrig and is now working on the projected Cynwyl extension.

Also in working order are three small Ruston-Hornsby 48hp 0-4-0 diesel-mechanical locomotives, and one North British 0-4-0 diesel-hydraulic locomotive. One other North British 0-4-0 diesel hydraulic locomotive is under repair.

The ex-Austin Motor Company 0-6-0 Pannier tank now named *Burtonwood Brewer* at Llangollen Station.

Opposite: No. 7828, **Odney Manor**, built at Swindon in 1950, and 0-6-0 Great Western tank locomotive just beyond the bridge in Llangollen Station

Llangollen Railway Society

Set in the valley of the River Dee, the Llangollen Railway is one of the most important restoration schemes and is the only standard-gauge steam line operating in North Wales. The line forms part of what was originally the Vale of Llangollen Railway opened in 1860 and running from Ruabon to Llangollen. By 1862, as the Llangollen & Corwen Railway, it had been extended to Corwen and in 1877 it reached Bala and Dolgellau. The Great Western Railway had always operated the line and absorbed it in 1896. For many years it operated successfully as a tourist line and for the carriage of goods, including slate from local quarries.

After the Second World War a decline set in because of the growth of car ownership and road haulage and in the early 1960s the Beeching Report recommended closure and this was scheduled for the latter part of 1965. In January 1965 the River Dee burst its banks, causing substantial damage and premature closure of the line, although the section from Ruabon to Llangollen remained in operation until 1968. The track was lifted and removed and the stations and other structures left to decay and vandalism.

***Odney Manor* at Berwyn Station, a superb black and white timbered building.**

There was strong local feeling that the famous Eisteddfod town of Llangollen should be able to support a steam railway, and in 1975 the Flint and Deeside Railway Preservation Society (now the Llangollen Railway Society) obtained what was initially a five-year lease on the land and buildings at Llangollen and the track-bed as far as Corwen. Restoration was carried out by a volunteer workforce. In 1981 a passenger service was started from Llangollen Station to Llangollen Goods Junction and subsequently to Berwyn Station, a distance of 2 miles. By Easter 1990 the line had been extended through the 680-yard Berwyn Tunnel to Deeside Halt, a total length of 4 miles. It is planned to extend the line in stages to Corwen as soon as possible. The first extension will be to Glyndyfdrwy Village, 5½ miles from Llangollen.

Llangollen Station, an attractive GWR building, has been superbly restored, as has the signal box at the end of Platform 1, and both the station and goods yard, which contains a good display of locomotives and rolling stock, are open to visitors. The station is in the town centre and there are car parks close by in Market Street. From Llangollen the line hugs the River Dee, crossing it by a stone and girder bridge, and begins the climb to Berwyn, characterized by its black and white timbered station building set on a rocky ledge above the river. Journeys can be broken here and only a short walk away are the Horse Shoe Falls and Telford's feeder canal. It is also possible to walk back to Llangollen, following the canal towpath. From Berwyn the line curves round a rock spur, gradually climbs up to Berwyn Tunnel and on emerging from the tunnel sweeps above the Dee, with superb views not possible from the main road, which runs above the railway, and into Deeside Halt. Here the visitor can either leave the train or wait for the return journey. The round trip takes around 50 minutes.

Apart from its own locomotive stock, details of which are given below, the line is frequently visited by preserved main-line steam locomotives. At some off-peak times trains are diesel-hauled. Carriage stock includes seven ex-British Rail Mk 1 coaches. There are many goods vehicles of varying types, together with an ex-British Rail Ransomes and Rapier 45-ton steam breakdown crane.

Photography: There is plenty of scope for photography at Llangollen Station and also from the road alongside Berwyn Station.

Other Attractions: Llangollen is the centre for the International Musical Eisteddfod. The town itself has a number of historic buildings. The River Dee is spanned by a 14th-century stone bridge and the town is overlooked by the remains of Castle Dinas Brau. Within easy distance are Telford's incomparable Pont Cysllte and Chirk aqueducts.

Services: Trains operate at weekends only in March, April, May, October, November and December, with full services during Easter and Spring Bank Holiday weeks, June to September and with 'Santa Special' Trains during the period up to Christmas. There are also special events during the year and 'Berwyn Belle Wine & Dine Trains'. For further information telephone 0978-860951 (24-hour talking timetable) or during office hours only (Monday to Friday) 0978-860979. Correspondence should be addressed to the Secretary, Llangollen Railway, The Station, Abbey Road, Llangollen, Clwyd, LL20 8SN.

Locomotives

5952 Cogan Hall	4-6-0

Ex-GWR and BR, built Swindon 1935. Privately owned.

7822 Foxcote Manor	4-6-0

Ex-GWR and BR, built Swindon 1950 and owned by the Foxcote Manor Society.

7828 Odney Manor	4-6-0

Ex-GWR and BR, built Swindon 1950. Privately owned

2859	2-8-0

Ex-BR and ex-Barry Scrapyard. Undergoing restoration.

5459 Burtonwood Brewer	**0-6-0 Saddle Tank**

Built by Kitson, Works number 5459, for the Austin Motor Company.

In addition an ex-BR, ex-NCB 0-6-0 pannier tank is undergoing restoration and there are a number of diesel locomotives.

Further Reading

Festiniog Railway

The Festiniog Railway, Vol. 1, *History and Route, 1800–1953;* Vol. 2, *Locomotive Rolling Stock and Quarry Feeders* by J. I. C. Boyd (The Oakwood Press, 1975)

Festiniog Railway Traveller's Guide (The Festiniog Railway Company, regularly updated)

The Little Wonder by John Winton (Michael Joseph, revised edition, 1986)

Snowdon Mountain Railway

Three Stops to The Summit by Rol Williams (Cyhoeddiad au Mei, 1990)

Talyllyn Railway

Railway Adventure by L. T. C. Rolt (David & Charles, revised edition, 1977)

Talyllyn Handbook (Talyllyn Railway Preservation Society, regularly updated)

The Talyllyn Railway by David Potter (David & Charles, 1990)

The Talyllyn Railway by J. I. C. Boyd (Wild Swan Publications, 1989)

Vale of Rheidol Railway

The Vale of Rheidol Light Railway by C. C. Green (Wild Swan Publications, 1986)

Welshpool & Llanfair Light Railway

The Welshpool & Llanfair Light Railway by Ralph Cartwright and R. T. Russell (David & Charles, 1989)